The Very Best Thing

BY KATIE WEAVER

JOYFUL GODDESS PRESS

2012

Joyful Goddess Press

ISBN: 0-6156-6440-7
ISBN-13: 9780615664408

DEDICATION

Dedicated to Merri Ann Brower, you were the best mother, friend and teacher that a girl could ever hope for. I love you and miss you every day.

A LETTER TO THE READER

In this beautifully diverse world that we are sharing, love is the answer. When we are tempted to judge other people and their choices, love is the answer. When other people are hurtful towards us, love is the answer. Love is always the answer. My hope for this book is that it will inspire you to love those that are easy to love and to love those who are difficult. When we approach all situations with love, our differences become our strengths. It is my deepest desire to see our society return to love in all that we do. I know that we can do it when we put our heads and our hearts together.

Love to you,

Katie

chapter 1

LUCY PULLED HER blanket a little tighter around her shoulders. Even in May, the air was very cool in Rocky Point, she thought. She was sitting on the hard metal bleachers watching her son, Luke, play baseball. The parents of the other kids were cheering loudly, as Brian hit the ball and ran the bases. Brian was a nice kid, she thought. His little sister Emily usually sat near Lucy and her daughter Hope. Lucy really liked Emily. She was a little bit younger than Hope, with long blond hair and big blue eyes. She was always at the game with Brian, but Lucy had never seen either of their parents at any of the games.

"Lucy, can I sit with you? I'm cold."

Lucy scooted over and made room for Emily in between her and Hope. The three snuggled together under a big red flannel quilt. Soon the game ended, and Luke came over to high five Hope.

"Come on Emily," said Brian, taking her by the hand. "Dad said he might be a few minutes late, and we should wait by the dugout."

Lucy watched the two children walk over to the dugout, wondering how late their father would be, and where their mother was. Soon, all of the other families and the coach had gone, leaving the children waiting quietly on the bench. Lucy was not comfortable leaving the children alone there, so she decided to wait with them.

"Luke, Hope, why don't you guys see if Brian and Emily would like to play on the slide with you for a little bit while they wait for their dad?" Soon, all four kids were running happily to the toys. Lucy pulled a book out of her bag to pass the time.

Thirty minutes went by, and their dad had still not arrived. Lucy was starting to wonder where he could possibly be. Finally, forty five minutes after the game had ended, a man pulled up in blue Camry. He was tall, at least 6 feet, Lucy guessed. He was dressed in a long sleeved light blue shirt, dark blue tie, and dark slacks. He walked out near the dugout.

"Are you Brian and Emily's dad?" Lucy called out, walking towards him.

"Yes, I am very late to pick them up. Have you seen them?" Doug was surprised by the woman who was addressing him. She was younger than him, he guessed, barely thirty. She was very petite, somewhere around 5'3, Doug estimated. She was wearing a tank top, a long tie dyed skirt and sandals. Very different from the way most of the conservative women in Rocky Point dressed.

"Yeah, they are playing on the toys with my kids. I hated to leave them alone, it is starting to get dark."

"Oh, wow, I really appreciate that. I had a late meeting at my office, and could not leave as soon as I thought that I would. I am sorry for making you wait. My name is Doug Brown, by the way," he said, extending his hand.

"Lucy Meriwether, my son Luke is on Brian's team," Lucy explained as she shook Doug's hand, looking up into his face. Wow, she thought, Emily looks just like him, blond hair and deep blue eyes.

By this time, the kids had spotted their dad, and were running up to greet him. As they were heading for the car, Doug turned.

"Thanks again Lucy, I really owe you one."

"No problem, it takes a village, right?" Lucy responded with a smile.

Once they were in the car, Brian chattered excitedly about the game all the way home. Doug was only half listening though. He was still thinking about the encounter he had just had with Lucy. She was so real, and so beautiful. She had dark eyes, and long, straight, chestnut brown hair, braided down her back. Doug thought that was a much nicer look than a lot of the women he knew from work or church who had chemically treated, spiky looking hair. Since his wife, Lisa, had died three years ago, Doug had not really done any dating. It wasn't until recently that he had even thought about women.

"It was really nice of Luke's mom to sit with you guys," he commented over dinner.

"Yeah, she is always nice," Emily said, swallowing a mouthful of macaroni and cheese. "Sometimes if I get cold at a game, she lets me sit with her in her blanket."

"She brings cookies or brownies or something to every game," Brian added.

Doug felt a twinge of guilt that he had missed so many of Brian's games, and vowed to make it to the next one.

ॐॐ

The next game was just two days away. Doug made a point of getting out of work a little early to come. When he and the kids arrived, he noticed that Lucy and her daughter were already sitting in the bleachers, watching the boys warm up. Trying to muster up some confidence, Doug sat down next to Lucy.

"Nice night for a game," he commented casually.

"Yes, the weather has been beautiful today," Lucy replied. "I am so glad that it is clear, so that I can enjoy the full moon tonight."

"Oh, sure," Doug said, puzzled about the full moon comment.

"Batter up!" called the umpire.

The game was very competitive, running much longer than usual. Suddenly Doug realized that he had a church meeting that he was already late for. He would just have to run the kids home now, and get over to the church. He leaned over to Emily.

"We are going to have to leave the game early, Em. I have a meeting at church. Run get your brother, so that I can get you home." Emily ran to get Brian.

"But dad, I can't leave now. Coach says if I am not here to bat, that the team will have to take an automatic out!" Brian pleaded.

"I am sorry son, but I made a commitment to the church. I have to get to my meeting." Doug felt bad, but knew that his pastor would not appreciate his lateness.

"Doug, I could take them home," Lucy said. "That way Brian can stay and finish the game."

"Oh, no, I could not possibly bother you again!"

"Really, it is no problem. Go ahead and get to your meeting." Lucy smiled with reassurance.

"Thanks Luke's mom!" Brian shouted as he sprinted back to the dugout with his team.

"Alright, I really appreciate this," Doug said, feeling a little awkward that Lucy was stepping in to save him, again.

⧙⧘

When the game was over, Lucy loaded all four kids into her old beetle, and drove to Doug's house with Brian's directions. When they pulled up to the curb, she noticed that the house was dark.

"Is your mother home?" she asked.

"We don't have a mom," Emily replied in her sweet, high pitched voice.

"Yes we do Emily," Brian growled. "Dad says she is with her Heavenly Father, that's all."

Lucy sucked in her breath. "Okay, well, Brian, honey, what do you guys usually do while your dad goes to meetings?"

"We make a peanut butter sandwich and watch TV until he gets home," Brian told her.

"How about we come in and wait with you for awhile?" Lucy felt so sorry for these kids with no mom. She hated to just drop them off to an empty house.

Once in the house, Lucy realized that the children had not eaten dinner. She sent the kids out back to play, and rummaged around in Doug's cupboards, trying to find something to make for dinner. She finally settled on pancakes and scrambled eggs. After the children were all fed, she helped them do their homework, and got Brian and Emily off to bed while her kids laid on the couch and watched TV.

"My dad always helps me to say my prayers before bed," Emily told Lucy as she tucked her in. "Can you help me?"

"Sure, I guess so. Who do you usually pray to Emily?"

"Jesus, silly, who else would I pray to? Sister Jones, my primary teacher, says that all kids have to pray to Jesus, to keep us safe and help us to be good and to forgive us of our sins." Emily knelt next to her bed and said a short prayer to Jesus. Lucy smiled, and tucked her blankets around her. She was wondering why in the world someone would want to teach this beautiful child that she was somehow a sinner, or that anything was wrong with her.

Lucy believed that all things happen for a reason, and she knew that these children had not just come into her life by chance. They needed her, and she knew it. She wondered how she could really be much of an influence in their lives, when their dad obviously had a very different view of the world than she did.

Shortly after ten, following a very tedious meeting, Doug pulled into his driveway. He noticed an old VW beetle sitting in front of his house. When he walked in the front door, there stood Lucy.

"Lucy!" he exclaimed, startled. "Why are you still here, is something wrong?"

"No, nothing is wrong. I just hated to leave the kids here alone. They have had dinner, and they are both in bed."

"Oh, I am really sorry. I did not mean for you to stay here with them. Now you had to keep your kids out so late. I feel really stupid about this." Doug was so embarrassed about the whole thing that he did not know what to say.

"Really Doug, it is no big deal. My kids have been asleep on the couch for a while now. You have some really great kids. I don't mind helping out at all." Lucy realized that Doug was feeling uncomfortable about her staying. "I'm sorry. I really didn't mean to intrude on your space."

"Oh, no! Please don't apologize to me. I am the one who has been inconsiderate. Actually, I am glad that you are here. I have been wanting to talk to you." Doug struggled to calm his nerves and to steady his shaky voice. "Do you want to sit on the patio and talk with me for a little bit?"

Lucy hesitated for a moment, wondering if she could trust Doug. He did not feel creepy to her, but she did not know him very well. She decided to trust her intuition.

"Sure, I would love to."

As they headed through the kitchen, Doug asked, "Can I get you something to drink?"

"Oh, yes, I would love a glass of wine," Lucy replied.

"Actually," Doug said awkwardly, "I don't drink."

"Oh, sorry, I would love a glass of water." Lucy wondered if she had offended Doug.

Doug's patio had two reclining chairs that both Lucy and Doug settled into. When Lucy sat and put her legs up, Doug noticed a tattoo on her right ankle that kind of looked like a star.

"Wow," Lucy sighed contentedly, "You have a beautiful view of the stars and the moon here."

Doug looked up. He had never really noticed. "You're right. The moon looks huge, doesn't it?"

"Yes, and the stars are so bright and clear. It is good for my soul," Lucy smiled dreamily, still looking at the stars. Doug was mesmerized with her. She was so beautiful and unique.

"What did you want to talk about, Doug?" Lucy asked, bringing him back to reality.

"Well, my kids seem to know you so well, and I hardly know you. I was just hoping to get a little better acquainted."

"Okay, I am an open book. What would you like to know?" Lucy smiled in the darkness, knowing that this conversation was going to get very interesting.

"Well, first of all, where are you from? I am sure that I have not seen you in Rocky Point until a few months ago." Doug was hoping to subtly find out if Lucy had a man in her life.

"I am from Denver. The kids and I moved here in February."

"That is a big change. Denver is a big city, and Rocky Point is barely on the map. Why did you come here, of all places?"

"I just needed life to slow down a little bit. I am trying to raise my kids to be socially responsible, and things in Denver were getting far from that. We needed wide open spaces to breathe. I like Rocky Point, because I can still drive into Denver for business when I need to. It is only forty minutes away."

"Speaking of business, what do you do for a living?" Couldn't be much, Doug thought, thinking of her beat up old car.

"I am a writer," Lucy answered simply.

"Really, a writer of what?"

"Books, mostly. Some internet stuff."

"You write books? Like published books?" Doug was trying to figure out why a published author would be living in Rocky Point, driving an old car, and voluntarily taking care of someone else's kids.

"Yeah, I have been published. I have four books out currently, and I am due to release my new one in the fall. I need to get busy on that one, to be honest. Anyways, it is my turn to ask some questions!"

"But wait, I want to know more about your books!" Doug protested.

"No way mister, I have things that I must know," laughed Lucy.

"Fine, fine," said Doug, "But we are coming back to you in a minute!"

"Alright, first of all, what do you do for a living?"

"I am an accountant. I work for a Denver firm."

"How old are you?"

"Thirty five," Doug said, wondering how old Lucy was. She looked so young.

"What is your favorite ice cream flavor?"

"Rocky road."

"Okay, how many siblings do you have?"

"I have two brothers. They both live here in Rocky Point with their wives and kids."

"That is nice, are you all close?"

"I guess so, but we are all busy. I see them at church and on holidays. Occasionally we get together. We used to all be great friends, we hung out a lot. Movies, bowling, that sort of thing."

"Why aren't you close anymore?"

"I don't really know. I guess it is probably my fault. When my wife, Lisa, died three years ago, I just stopped hanging out with anyone. I couldn't stand to have fun, to laugh, to do anything that reminded me of her....." Doug fell into silence for a few minutes.

Finally Lucy said, "I'm sorry Doug, I did not mean to dredge up bad memories."

"No, it's okay, they are not bad memories. I think that it is my turn to ask now, if you don't mind." Doug tried to lighten the mood, hating that he had turned into such a downer.

"Alright, my books. I write in the new age arena."

"I'm sorry, but I really have no idea what you are talking about," Doug admitted. New age, what was that?

"Well, I write about crystals, herbs, energy healing, vibrations, astrology, and things like that." It was not so much that Lucy was ashamed of who she was, but making friends in this Christian town had been tough. She knew that when she told Doug that she was Pagan, and that her books were all about Pagan and Wiccan practices, he may not give her a second thought. It seemed like the people in this town were holding on to some very old ideas that Pagans were devil worshipers. An insane thought, really, since Pagans don't even believe in the devil.

At that moment, the back door opened, and Emily emerged, crying. "Dad, I threw up. My tummy really hurts!"

Doug leapt from his chair and picked Emily up. "Oh, sweetie, I am so sorry you are not feeling well. Did you make it to the bathroom?"

"No, I threw up in my bed, all over my favorite blanket and my teddy bears," Emily sobbed.

Lucy reached out for Emily. "Here, I will help Emily while you take care of her bed."

Doug nodded and headed for Emily's room. When he was done cleaning up and remaking Emily's bed, he found Emily and Lucy in the kitchen. Emily was wrapped snugly in a quilt, drinking from a mug.

"I picked a little mint from your flower bed and made her some tea for her tummy," Lucy told Doug. "She should be feeling better."

"What, why mint tea?"

"Mint is a naturally cooling herb. It is excellent for stomach issues," Lucy explained.

"Oh, I did not even realize that I had mint out there. I do have some of the pink stuff in the cupboard for stomach aches."

"Pink stuff?" Lucy asked.

"Yeah, you know, pink stuff. Pepto bismol?"

Lucy looked blank.

"It is medicine. For stomach aches," Doug was dumbfounded. How could anyone not know what Pepto is?

"Oh, I see. I don't use pharmaceuticals, I guess that is why I didn't know what the 'pink stuff' is."

"You don't use any pharmaceuticals? Why? And what do you do when you get sick? Surely you have to take some medicine from time to time?" Doug was having a hard time believing this. Why would anyone avoid medicine, anyway?

"Nope, I don't ever take medicine. My kids don't either. I make my own medicine with herbs if we need something, but it is pretty rare that I do that, either." Lucy could see from Doug's face that he was really confused. "It is just a personal choice, Doug. I don't like the way medicine makes me feel. It interferes with my intuition and overall feeling of well being. I also believe that wellness has many forms, and western medicine is only one of them." With that Lucy, kissed Emily on the forehead, and said, "It is really getting late. I had better get going. I will see you at the next game, okay?"

Once Lucy had her kids back home and settled in their beds, she wandered out into her own backyard to enjoy the full moon and the cool spring air. "What am I doing," she wondered? "Doug is not my type at all. How can I be attracted to a Christian? This will never work. Still, he feels so familiar to me."

chapter 2

DOUG HAD A hard time concentrating the next day at work. All he could think about was Lucy, and the amazing, strange events of the previous night. Full moons, herbs for medicine, books about the 'New Age'. Who was this woman? Doug was intrigued with her in a way that a teen is intrigued with someone who their parents have forbidden them to date. He knew she may go against everything that his religion and life had taught him, but still, he had to know more.

As soon as his kids were in bed, Doug signed onto the internet. He ran a search for Lucy Meriweather. Dozens of pages popped up. He clicked on one page titled, "Lucy Meriweather, biography".

Lucy Meriweather is a leading author in the New Age field. She has written many articles and four books dealing with Pagan and Wiccan practices. In addition to her writings, Ms. Meriweather is a practicing wiccan. She belongs to the oldest Coven in Denver, CO. She is well known for her skills in energy healing and herbal healing. Ms. Meriweather is a full time mother of two......

Doug felt like he had been kicked in the stomach. A witch? He was falling for a witch? Not now. He knew that his family, his church, even his community would not tolerate this. He had to end his feelings for Lucy now.

Lucy headed to the next baseball game feeling a little nervous. She had no idea how Doug would respond to her. To her surprise, neither Doug, nor his children showed up. Lucy was both concerned that there might be something wrong, and angry at the thought that maybe she was the something that was wrong.

The following day, while the children were in school, Lucy drove to Denver to meet some friends for lunch. It was nice to get together with people who knew her well. These women were the closest thing to family that Lucy had. Her mother had been a witch. A very talented witch, in fact, but not much of a mother to her. When Lucy was 10, her mother left her in the care of Tina, the high priestess of her coven, to go on a "spiritual journey" to "find" herself. That was the last time Tina or Lucy ever heard from her.

Tina raised Lucy through those awkward teenage years, guiding her spiritual growth and paying for an excellent education at an elite private school in Denver. Lucy wanted to go to public school, but Tina would not hear of it. She remembered the conversation well. "But Tina, only nerds and bookworms go to private school!" Tina had laughed, "Nonsense, smart people go to private school, and you, my dear are very bright. You would get lost in the chaos of a public high school. Besides, I have a lot of traveling to do this next year, and with the private school's 'work at your own pace' policy, you can come with me, and not get behind. It is perfect, you'll see!" And so it was. Lucy graduated from high school when she was barely seventeen, and had gone on to the Metropolitan State College of Denver, where she graduated with her bachelors degree in English with a focus on writing. While she attended day classes at the Met, she also attended night classes at the College of Wicca and Old Lore on the other side of Denver. The colleges meshed nicely for her. She loved the liberal thinking of the Met, and enjoyed her classes. The College of Wicca was fascinating and filled up her spiritual side.

In her last semester at the Met, Lucy was required to write her senior paper, a 200 page dissertation on the subject of her choosing. Her paper was titled, "A practical guide of Wicca". Her professor raved about her work, telling her that he had not enjoyed a student paper that much in a long time. Two months after graduation, she received a call from her professor. He had been telling a friend of his, an editor, about her unique senior dissertation. The editor, Suzanne, was interested in reading it. Lucy met with her the very next day. Two weeks later, Suzanne called Lucy with very good news. Her firm wanted to publish Lucy's paper as a book! Tina was so proud of Lucy that she threw a big party with the whole coven to celebrate.

"Hey Lucy," Amber broke into her thoughts. "You have not had much to say today. What is going on with you?" Lucy figured that it would be hard to hide her feelings from Amber. Amber was an empath, which means that she feels the emotions of other people around her. Lucy could relate, since she, too, was empathic sometimes. It could be very uncomfortable to be in a large crowd of people and start feeling very sad, angry, ill and worried all at the same time, for no reason at all. Tina had helped Lucy learn to block the empathic feelings when she was in Junior High school. She usually only used her empath skills when she was doing energy work on people, so that she could accurately help them with her pain and health issues.

Lucy squirmed a little, not sure that she wanted to bring it up. "Oh, nothing, just feeling a little bit down, I guess."

"Well, no kidding," said Megan sitting right across from her. "Your chakras are all out of whack, particularly your solar plexus. What could have happened to shake you so much?"

Lucy had to smile at this. Megan was an Aura Reader, which meant that she can see people's energy systems that are around their bodies. The solar plexus is the third chakra, near the belly button. It is usually yellow. Self esteem and self worth are centered here.

"Dang, I can't hide anything from you guys! It is about this guy in Rocky Point," Lucy began.

"Ooooooh, of course it is," Megan laughed. "Go on."

"Well, his name is Doug. His son is on Luke's baseball team. Fate has thrown me together with his kids, Brian and Emily twice now. The second time I ended up at their house watching them until Doug got home from a meeting. When he got home we sat out on his deck, watched the stars, and talked. We really hit it off. There is something that feels so familiar about him that I cannot shake it."

"That sounds really great, Lus. You haven't had a man in your life since who knows when? Why is this a problem?" asked Tina. Lucy knew that Tina worried about her being alone all the time.

"But you want it to work, I can tell," protested Amber. Lucy shot her a dirty look.

"Get out of my head Amber!" She shouted, throwing a napkin at her smirking friend. "It just really cannot work between us. He is a devout Christian."

"WHAT?" Megan squeaked, choking on her iced tea. "A Christian? Why would you even entertain the thought of hooking up with a Christian?"

"I don't know," Lucy sighed. "Maybe this small town life that I thought I wanted is getting to me. I am getting really lonely. Anyways, it does not matter. He must have googled me by now. He and his kids have stopped showing up at baseball games, avoiding me entirely."

"Well, Lucy, for what it is worth," Tina admonished, "If he feels so familiar to you, there may be a reason. Don't be so quick to judge him on his religion. You don't appreciate it when people do the same thing to you. Just trust your intuition, and you will figure it all out."

"Thanks Tina, I will remember that," Lucy knew very well that when Tina shared some wisdom with her, it made a lot of sense to listen. Tina was a seer, and often saw into the future. Not only that, Lucy suspected that Tina knew her better than she knew herself sometimes.

"Expect the best and the very best thing will work out." Lucy smiled at Tina's words. She had been saying that phrase to her for as long as Lucy could remember.

"Speaking of Rocky Point, I am still planning on having you all out for the Summer Solstice celebration," Lucy said, hoping to change the subject. "I have a few spare rooms, if anyone wants to stay over. I have been collecting fallen logs for a while now, from the woods behind my house. There is an awesome spot for a bonfire."

"Sure, Lucy, we are planning on it," said Tina.

"I can't wait to see your new house," added Megan. "Didn't you say that it is really old?"

"Yeah, it was built in 1904," said Lucy. "It is a big old rock farm house. You will really love the kitchen and the garden. My house makes it worth living in Rocky Point."

෧✑

That night, Lucy had a hard time getting to sleep. Tina had told her to trust her intuition on the matter. At the moment, her intuition was being overruled by her head, telling her Christians and Pagans do not hook up. Finally, she decided to cast a dream spell. "After all, when I am asleep, my subconscious, or right brain, takes over, allowing me to see exactly what my intuition wants me to see. My ego, or left brain, is powerless there," Lucy thought. She climbed out of bed, pulled a robe on over her satin night gown, and ventured downstairs to her altar room. "I am so lucky," she mused, "that I have a room just for worship and practicing the craft. I love being able to come in here and do whatever I need to do."

Lucy used her athame, a short small dagger-like knife, to cast a circle, calling in the elements of fire, water, air, earth, and then the four directions, north, east, south, and west and the great unknown, the ether. She placed a bit of incense in a tiny cast iron cauldron on the altar, and lit it with a match to get it smoldering. Next she anointed a small silver candle with clove oil, lit it, and spoke, *"I call upon all of the beings of light and love associated with this silver candle energy to guide my heart and intuition with knowingness and trust. I ask my intuition to come through to me in the form of a dream, that I may understand the messages sent to me."* After which Lucy sat with the candle until it burned down, released the circle, and went to bed, falling quickly to sleep.

ॐ∾

On the other side of town, Doug was also still wide awake. He still could not get Lucy out of his head. "How have I become so attached to this woman, I have only ever met her twice? I am just lonely, that must be it. Maybe this is just a sign that I am ready to start dating again. Maybe I should ask one of the single women at church out on a date... Yeah, that must be it. It is not Lucy that I am drawn to. It is the thought of having a woman around. Tomorrow I will figure out who to call, and ask one of them out." Finally sleep came to Doug as well.

ॐ∾

Fate is a funny thing. Once it has decided that two people should be together, it is very persistent. That was the case with that windy, rainy night in Rocky Point. The wind swirled and howled, bringing dreams that could not be ignored.....

chapter 3

LUCY WOKE WITH a start to the sound of booming thunder shaking the house. She looked at the clock, 4:30. "What an amazing dream," she thought. She snapped on the lamp, grabbed her dream journal and a pen from her night-stand, and began writing.

Tonight I had an amazing dream. It was another time, maybe the 1700's, in France. I lived in a small village. I was very happy. I had a beautiful little cottage, with flowers and gardens. I had children, several of them. I raised chickens and traded the eggs for other commodities. The most amazing part was my husband. He made me wildly happy. He was always there, holding me, kissing me, sitting under the stars with me. We had a wonderful life. He looked so familiar to me, it seems like I know him in this life...

Lucy gasped and dropped the notebook into her lap, the image of Doug's face still fresh in her mind.

ॐॐ

Doug slept later than usual, grateful that it was Sunday. As he readied himself and his kids for church, he thought about his pledge to ask someone from church out on a date. His confidence was already starting to wane. "Maybe I should wait and ask my brothers about this before I get the whole church gossiping about me," he reasoned. He knew that his family would all meet at his parents house for their usual Sunday lunch after church.

Even though he usually avoided these gatherings, he decided that he had better go this time. He needed some advice.

The church service went by quickly enough, though Doug did not pay very much attention. He was too busy scanning the room, looking for prospective dates. After church he and the kids drove over to his parents house. The smell of pork roast in the oven filled Doug's nose as he and the kids walked into the back door. His mother was already home from church and shaping rolls at the counter.

"Well Doug, this is a nice surprise," his mother Cheryl said, standing on tiptoe to kiss him on the cheek. "Are you guys staying for lunch?"

"If you have enough. I know you weren't planning on us," Doug replied.

"We always have enough for you, silly," Doug's mother was so happy to have him and the kids over for lunch. She wondered if this meant he was finally starting to feel more like himself.

Just then, the back door burst open and her other two sons, David and Brandon, plus their wives and children came in. The kids all squealed with delight to see each other, and sprinted to the backyard to play. Everyone was pleasantly surprised to see Doug and the kids. He had been so distant with all of them since Lisa died. They had all tried to help him, but he pushed them all back. He did not want his mother or sisters in law to feel like they had to take over raising his kids. He knew that they were his responsibility, and he was willing to accept that. After all, the busier the kids kept him, the less time he had to focus on the huge hole in his heart.

"Why don't you guys play some basketball while I finish up the rolls?" Cheryl suggested to her sons. She knew that a little bonding time would do them all some good.

"I will referee," volunteered Bob, Doug's dad.

"Sure you will, old man," laughed David. "From your lawn chair!"

"You know it!" Bob replied, slapping David on the back.

After thirty minutes of street ball, the men stopped for a breather.

"So Doug," Brandon panted, "What brings you around today?"

"Why?" Doug asked, grabbing the basketball from Brandon and shooting. "Can't a guy come hang out with his family for no reason at all?"

"Yeah, sure. It is just that you have been absent so much the last while, I just wondered." Brandon was thrilled to have his brother around. They had all worried about him so much. Since Lisa died, Doug had been like a robot. Go to work, go home. Go to church, go home. No social life at all. He still held positions in the church, but did what was asked of him quietly, offered no opinions.

"Well, you got me, actually. I have been thinking about dating again, and needed some advice." Doug felt weird even saying those words.

"Whohoooo!" Brandon bellowed.

"What is so exciting over here?" David approached, wiping his brow.

"Doug is ready to date again, he wants some advice," Brandon informed him.

"Wow, Doug, that is really great news," said David, clapping him on the back.

Just then, Cheryl leaned out the back door and called the men in for lunch. The dining room was full of tantalizing smells. Rolls, roasted pork, mashed potatoes, and apple pie, hot out of the oven. When they were all seated, Bob offered a blessing on the food. After the prayer, everyone passed around dishes and platters, filling their plates. Doug was really glad that he had come. Not only was he really enjoying such a wonderful meal, his children were acting very happy to be around their family.

"What did you all think of the sermon today?" Asked Bob. "It gave me a lot to think about."

"Me too," said Brandon's wife, Liz. "When the pastor was talking about how Jesus loved everyone, and did not hold anyone in judgment, it made me think about how often I judge people on the street or in the grocery store just because of the way that they look."

"Yeah," said Brandon, "But I think that you still have to be careful. There are freaks out there, you know. In our church, it is a sin to tattoo your body, smoke, and drink alcohol. When I see people like that, it is hard for me not to put them down."

"I know what you mean," David chimed in. "Maybe it is not okay to judge them. But I sure do not have to like them or socialize with them!"

Doug felt like a lead weight had been dropped in his stomach. He was thinking about the night that Lucy had asked for a glass of wine, and about the tattoo he had noticed on her ankle. Some sort of symbol, he was not sure what.

"What if we are missing out on some really great people by refusing to consort with those who do not share our beliefs, though?" Asked David's wife, Nicole.

"So what if we are? In my book, if you roll around with the pigs, you are bound to get dirty." David retorted.

"I agree," Brandon chimed in. "I can't see any reason to consort with people like that."

Doug excused himself to the bathroom. He sat on the edge of the tub, trying to get his thoughts clear. Obviously, he had made the right choice, trying to forget about Lucy. His brother's comments still bothered him though. Lucy was the kindest person he had ever met. Just being near her made him better, somehow. It was not fair that just because of her personal beliefs, that others would see her as something so bad. He was suddenly feeling very protective of her. "What is my problem?" He wondered. "I don't have any feelings for Lucy anyway!" That was the problem though. He did have feelings for Lucy, and he could not just cast them aside. How could he? Doug splashed his face with cold water, and returned to dinner, determined to get through dinner amicably.

"So, Doug," Cheryl began, "Brandon was just telling us that you are ready to get back out there and date again. That is wonderful news!"

Doug groaned, and hissed "Big mouth!" to Brandon.

"Oh, you don't have to be mad," Brandon laughed. "It is good news!"

"Ooooh, Doug, one of our neighbors is single. She works in the primary at church. Maybe you know her, Sister Smith?" asked Liz.

"Sister Smith? Isn't she a little old for me?" Asked Doug, shuddering. Sister Smith had to be at least 15 years his senior.

"Okay, maybe. What about the organist. She is single. I think that her name is Sister Price, right?" Chimed in David.

Again, Doug groaned.

"Well, what are you looking for in a woman, honey. Maybe that would help us to narrow down the field," asked his mother helpfully.

By this time, Doug had the full attention of everyone at the table, including his own kids. "Well, she needs to be younger than me, and pretty. I want her to have some kids of her own, and to be a good mother. Someone who is kind, nurturing. That sort of thing. And long hair, I really like long hair."

"Dad!" Emily shouted. "I know who you should date. It is Lucy! It has to be! She sounds just like that!"

"Yeah, dad!" Added Brian. "You like her, and she is a great cook!"

The table fell silent as all adults in the room turned to stare at Doug. Doug's face flushed red. "Uh, well, no guys. Sorry. Lucy and I just don't have enough in common to really date."

"But dad," Emily protested, "She has two kids, and she is super nice to us. Plus she is beautiful, and kind. Remember the other night when she fixed my tummy ache with some leaves from outside? I really want you to date her dad!" Emily's pitch was getting higher, like she was starting to get upset. "Why won't you?"

By this time, there were a lot of questions being fired at Doug from the whole table, such as "Who is she? Where does she live? Have I seen her at church? How long have you known her?"

"Okay, okay, slow down people!" Doug took a deep breath, then told the whole story of how he met Lucy, what she was doing in Rocky Point, and why she had been at his house. He avoided the entire religion issue, however.

"Well, I am thoroughly confused," said Nicole. "It sounds to me like she is made for you. How can you say that you have nothing in common?"

"We just don't, that's all," said Doug sullenly.

"But dear, I can hear it in your voice. You do have feelings for her," his mother insisted.

Doug eyed his children, who were both still watching him expectantly. "Why don't all of you kids go out and play for a little bit until dessert?"

"That is a good idea," Liz said, ushering all of the kids out into the backyard.

"The truth is, she is everything that I have ever wanted in many ways. I can't stop thinking about her. But I can't have her. I don't really even want to tell you all why. But trust me, you would be very unhappy with me if I were to pursue a relationship with her." Doug dropped his eyes to the table.

"How can that be? She sounds perfect!" Exclaimed David. "Oh, wait, I think I know what the problem is. Is she married?"

"No, of course not!"

"Then what?" Liz was getting impatient.

"She is just different from me. Her religion is different." Doug was wondering how he could make a quick exit.

"Oh, really? Well, what is she, Catholic?" Bob asked.

"Uh, no, not Catholic." Doug suppressed a smile, thinking about how his family might react if they knew the truth.

"Well, maybe you could use this as a missionary opportunity. See if you can get her to come to church with you, Doug," suggested Nicole.

To this, Doug laughed out loud, thinking about how that phone conversation would go. *"Hi Lucy, it's me, Doug. Hey, I was wondering if you would like to reverse your entire belief system and come to church with me on Sunday? I promise no one will try to stone you to death."*

"Alright everyone, I think that we have hassled poor Doug enough! No wonder he never comes over," Cheryl admonished, smiling at Doug.

ॐ✎

Sunday was an altogether different day for Lucy. After sleeping in, she took a long, hot bath. Then she made a cup of coffee, and headed out into the garden to meditate. After an hour of communing with nature, Lucy's soul felt renewed. She fed her chickens, gathered a few eggs, and headed into the house to wake her kids and make breakfast.

"Out of bed, sleepy heads!" She sang into their bedrooms.

Soon two pajama clad kids came wandering out of their rooms and into the kitchen. Lucy served them each a veggie omelet and a mug of tea. After breakfast, everyone headed out to work in the garden. It was good for Lucy to see all of the new life springing up around her. Last night's rain had left her yard smelling so clean and new. Big, fat raindrops hung from flower petals. The lettuce, radishes, peas, and spinach were all getting big, along with lots of new things starting to sprout. By noon, the garden was weeded, and they were all hot and tired. Lucy made up a tray of sandwiches and lemonade. She and the kids ate lunch under and ancient willow tree. As they chewed in silence, Lucy wondered at the peaceful, calm energy radiating from her children.

Hope broke the silence, "Mom, it seems like this old tree is speaking to me."

"Really? What is it saying to you?" Lucy loved watching her kids grow into their spiritual selves, with their intuition growing all the time.

"He says that he has seen many children live and grow up here. He likes us. He is glad that we are here." Hope looked dreamy, resting her head on the massive trunk.

"That is wonderful Hope. This would be a good spot for you to spend some time being quiet, meditating every day." Lucy was carefully cultivating her children's gifts, without pressuring or over-instructing them. Moments like these were priceless to her.

After lunch Lucy headed into her office to work on her new book for a little bit, while Hope and Luke played outside. Lucy was getting a bit nervous about the new book. She was on a deadline with her publisher that she was afraid that she could not meet. Every idea that she started on ended up hitting a brick wall. Today, though, her thoughts kept wandering back to the dream she had the night before. Finally, she gave up on brainstorming for the new book, and typed out her dream instead, trying to remember as many details as possible.

"Mom," Luke called, knocking on the door, "Will you take me to the park to practice batting at the baseball diamond?"

Lucy sighed, wishing that she had gotten more done. "Sure, son. I'll meet you in the car in five minutes!"

⁊⋙

"Bye Gramma, bye Grandpa!" Doug's kid's called as they climbed into the car.

"Come back soon, all of you!" Cheryl waved as they backed out of the driveway.

"It was good to have Doug here," Bob commented to Cheryl as Doug drove away. "I am curious about this woman, Lucy."

"Me too," Cheryl agreed. "I think that I might have to go to a baseball game here soon," she said to Bob with a wink.

⁊⋙

Doug wondered if this day had been helpful for him at all. He had not decided on any women from his church to date. His brothers had made it pretty clear that they would not support someone like Lucy, yet his sisters in law had urged him to date Lucy. Ugh, what to do?

"Lucy!" Emily screamed from the back seat.

"What? Where?" Doug jumped with a start.

"There, with Hope and Luke, playing baseball. Can we join them Dad, please? I have my gear in the trunk, and I really need to practice!" Brian begged.

Doug wanted to keep driving, but something made him stop. "Alright, but only for a few minutes."

"Yay!" Yelled the kids as they scrambled out of the car.

Doug walked out to the baseball diamond, where Lucy was pitching overhand to Luke. Is there anything this woman can't do?

"Hi Lucy, hi Hope, hi Luke! We were just driving past, and my kids were hoping that you guys would let us in on your game. Would that be okay?"

"Sure," Luke called. "We could use a few more players. This will be fun!"

By then, Emily and Brian were already on the field, hugging Lucy, and high fiving her kids. Doug felt a twinge of guilt, realizing how happy it would make his kids to have Lucy in their lives. No, Doug, stop it. You have to learn to be friends with her without being attracted to her that's all there is too it, he chided himself.

Doug grabbed a mitt, and assumed the catcher position behind home plate. Lucy continued to pitch. Doug was amazed at how hard she could throw the ball. He was amused by the fact that she was playing baseball in a long skirt and bare feet.

Lucy wondered why fate kept putting her and Doug together. She was quite sure that there could not really be a romantic relationship here. After all, they were much too different. But, still, every time she turned around, another meeting with him presented itself.

The game lasted close to an hour. They were all laughing and teasing, making awkward attempts to get people out on base. The kids were all having a blast. Even Emily and Hope got to bat. Finally, everyone took a break in the grass. Doug marveled at the easy way that Lucy laughed and joked with all of the kids. He knew he wasn't the most fun dad ever, feeling really stiff with his kids most of the time.

"Well, guys," Lucy said, "We had better get going. We still have not had dinner."

"Oh, mom, can Emily and Brian and their dad come home with us for dinner?" Hope begged. "Please, please, please?"

Lucy paused, wondering what the right thing to do was. Her home was filled with reminders of who she was. Her alter room, crystals, fairies, sculptures everywhere. If they came to her house, there was no going back from that.

"Please, mom? I really want to show Brian my room," added Luke.

Doug shifted uncomfortably. He actually felt himself really wanting to go, but knowing full well what a bad idea it was.

Lucy, on the other hand, was getting tired of the universe taunting her. She decided that she might as well get this over with. If she and Doug were really meant for each other, then he was going to have to know the truth about her. "Besides," she reasoned to herself, "I have nothing to hide. I am who I am, and I am proud of that. No more hiding!"

"I think that would be wonderful! What do you think, Doug?"

"Well, uh, I guess that it would be okay. Are you sure you want company on this short of notice?" Doug wanted to kick himself. He seemed to have no power to say no.

"Sure. Why don't you follow me?" With that, Lucy jumped up nimbly and headed for her car.

chapter 4

LUCY'S HOUSE TURNED out to be on the outskirts of town, on a beautiful wooded acre. Doug cringed when he realized that she lived a few doors down from the pastor of his church, and that several other people from his congregation lived around her as well. He hoped no one would recognize his car.

The second the car stopped, his kids jumped out and headed to the backyard with Luke and Hope.

"Wow," Doug muttered to himself. "This place must be a hundred years old. Why does an accomplished author live in an ancient house and drive an ancient car? She must not be all that popular." Doug was quickly impressed with the beauty of Lucy's home, however. Giant old trees surrounded her property. Wildflowers grew up where ever they wanted to. Her flower beds were filled with honeysuckle, wisteria, and a number of flowers that Doug could not identify. Climbing vines were edging their way up the old rock home. Doug walked up the stone staircase to the covered patio that ran across the front of the house. There was a porch swing to his left with a flannel blanket resting on it, inviting someone to come and relax there. Right next to the front door was a giant pointed white and mostly clear rock. It was at least as big as his head. It came to a point, that faced the doorway. Doug knew that it must have some purpose, but he could not imagine what. Suddenly, he grew a bit nervous. What all was Lucy into, anyway?

At that moment, his thoughts were broken when Lucy walked up behind him and said, "That is a clear quartz point. A giant crystal."

"It is very impressive," Doug admitted. "Why do you keep it outside?"

Lucy decided to be honest and open. "Well, clear quartz is known for its ability to clear energy. I keep this one by the front door to clear people's energy before they enter my house, keeping my home clear of negativity."

"Really? Does it really work?" What is she talking about, he wondered? How could a rock remove energy from people?

"Yes, it does a great job. I mined this crystal myself on a crystal gathering excursion in Arkansas a couple of years ago."

"You did? I had no idea that we had that kind of stuff in the United States."

"Oh, yeah, the US is full of crystals," Lucy told him. "The woman who raised me, Tina, is a geologist. When I was younger, I traveled all over the world with her mining all kinds of rocks and minerals."

With that, Lucy opened the front door, and gestured him inside. He looked sideways at the crystal as he walked past, wondering what it was going to do to him.

After they entered, Doug blinked, trying to get accustomed to the low light of the room. It looked more like a museum gallery than a living room. There were statues and sculptures everywhere. Doug walked over to get a closer look at a four foot tall gray statue in a corner. It was a beautiful woman with a long flowing gown and long wavy hair. In her hand she was wielding a dagger. "That is Badb," Lucy told him. "The Irish Goddess of war."

Next he approached a smaller statue. This one looked Egyptian to him. "That one is Isis, the Goddess of magic, healing, feminine power, and eternal life."

"Are they all Goddesses?" Doug asked, gesturing around.

"Yes, all Goddesses."

Doug was amazed by all of the Goddesses in the room. He could have spent all night examining them.

Lucy motioned him over to her antique, red velvet couch. "Doug, I have not been completely forthcoming with you, and I think that I need to fix that," she began. "When I told you that I am an author in the new age field, that was not as accurate as it could have been. The truth is, I am an author in Pagan and Wiccan studies. In fact, I practice Wicca. The truth is, I am a witch."

Doug nodded, numbly. Of course he already knew all of this information, but it was still odd hearing it come straight from her. "Actually, Lucy, I already knew that. I googled you after that night at my house."

Lucy laughed out loud. Of course! She had suspected as much. All of this stressing out, when Doug already knew the truth. Then the reality of the matter struck her. "But then, if you already know that I am a witch, why are you here? I thought that you would not want anything to do with me."

"Why would you think that?" Doug asked, wondering if he was really that transparent.

"Well, you are obviously a Christian. Your house is full of pictures of Jesus, scriptures, stuff like that. Usually Christians don't consort with Wiccans, so I am just surprised, that's all."

"Well," Doug replied nervously. "I don't really know. My kids really like you, and it has been a long time since I have seen them so happy. I know that it sounds kind of silly now, but at first I thought that maybe you and I could have a romantic relationship. Crazy, huh?"

"Yeah," Lucy laughed, relieved. "Crazy. Who could imagine it, a Witch and a Christian."

"Totally insane," Doug agreed. "But that does not mean we can't be friends, right? For our kids sake." Doug hated the bitter taste in his mouth that the word 'friends' left.

"Sure, right. For the kids," Lucy agreed. She bit back a bit of regret. Something inside of her was telling her there had to be more there than that, but she decided to go with the friendship thing for now.

Later on, after a filling meal of quiche and salad, the kids went up to play in their bedrooms while dessert baked in the oven. Doug helped Lucy wash up the dishes in the big farmhouse kitchen.

"So, Doug, tell me more about your religion," Lucy said. "I love learning new things."

"Well, okay. Obviously you know that I am Christian. My church believes that Christ died on the cross to atone for our sins."

"Really?" Asked Lucy, puzzled. "What sins?"

"You know, sins. All of the stuff people do that is bad, I guess. The big ones, like killing, stealing, rape, adultery, for starters."

"Sure, but those are all social taboos, as well," Lucy pointed out.

"That is true,"" Doug agreed. "But there are a lot more. Smoking, drinking, swearing, jealousy, impure thoughts, sex outside of marriage, lying, worshiping false idols, to name a few."

"Wow, sounds like a lot of things are considered a sin. What happens if you commit one of these 'sins'?" Lucy was wondering how anyone avoids all of these behaviors, all the time.

"If it is minor stuff, then you are supposed to pray to Jesus to forgive you. If it is major stuff, you have to go talk to the pastor and admit what you have been up to. He will come up with a suitable punishment for you. Otherwise, you run the risk of going to hell when you die."

"Oh, wow. Sounds really strict." Lucy was amazed at how limiting Doug's religion was, but was trying not to be rude. "I am confused about one thing though. If Jesus has already atoned for your sins, why do you have to repent for them?"

Doug stared at her, wondering what the answer was to this question. "Uh, well, I guess that it is a respect thing, more than anything else. I have actually never thought about it before," Doug admitted.

"Hmmm, interesting. I am sure I will have lots more questions after I ponder this. Thanks for sharing with me."

"Mom!" Hope interrupted, limping into the room. "I fell off of my bed and hurt my leg. Can you make it stop hurting?"

"Sure, sweetie, come over here and sit." Hope sat on the floor in front of Lucy and raised her leg up onto Lucy's lap. Lucy put both palms on Hope's leg, closed her eyes, and took a deep breath. She held that posture for two or three minutes, looking very serene. Then she opened her eyes, shook her hands and smiled at Hope. "Is that better?"

"Yep," Hope called as she jumped up and ran back upstairs. "Thanks, mom!"

"Whoa, what was that?" Doug asked, wondering what in the world he had just witnessed.

"That was energy healing. I put my hands over the hurt, called on universal energy to pass through me and out of my hands, then closed my eyes and allowed it to happen. The energy passed through me and into Hope where she was hurt, and healed her." Lucy made it all sound so simple. "Kind of like a blessing."

"But how do you know that it is working?" Doug was really having a hard time grasping this idea, but Lucy was so sincere, that he couldn't help think that there must be something to it.

"Well, in the results, obviously. Hope limped in here hurting, and then ran out like nothing ever happened a few minutes later," Lucy pointed out.

"Of course, but how do you know, while you are doing it, that the energy is moving through?"

"Oh, that is easy. I feel it. My hands get really hot and tingly. There is also a spot in the small of my back that gets warm and feels like it is pulsing." Lucy knew that she was exposing some really different ideas to Doug. She also knew that she needed to be herself, and hoped that she wasn't scaring him off.

"Okay, I am definitely going to need some time to process all of that. Can I ask you some other questions about your beliefs?" Doug was so curious, he had to know more. This stuff was a completely different world than he ever thought existed.

"Sure, fire away!"

"Well, first of all, is it really true that witches worship the devil?"

Lucy burst out laughing, giggling until she was gasping for breath. "Nope, not at all. That rumor was started by the Catholic church hundreds of years ago. It is so funny to me, because we don't even believe in the devil. Or hell, for that matter."

"Really?" Doug was both relieved and incredulous at the same time.

"Really. We worship the Goddess, who is the mother of all things. She is the creator, and the beginning and ending of all things."

"Wow, that is a big difference from Christianity. Do you also worship a God?"

"We do. The God is a consort to the Goddess, and a co-creator. He is a vital companion to her, since it takes female and male to create."

"Okay, that makes sense, but you don't believe in hell? But without the fear of hell, what keeps people from committing terrible acts all the time?"

"Wiccans believe that they are responsible for their own actions. They believe in Karma, which basically means that their actions now will have a direct impact on their future, whether that means this life, or their next life."

"The next life?" Doug inquired, curious.

"Well sure. We couldn't possibly learn everything that we need to know in one life. We believe that we have many lives. Some male lives, some female lives, with many different opportunities for growth."

"Wow," Doug said, thinking for a minute. "So, in other words, Karma encourages people to follow the rules, because they don't want to have to pay for bad behavior in another life, right?"

"Well, kind of, but there aren't really 'rules'. Most covens do have some sort of Wiccan Rede that they follow, but it can be interpreted differently by different people."

"But then, how do you know what is expected of you?"

Lucy took him by the hand, "Let me show you." She led him into a room off of the living room, where a table laden with a lot of curious items stood in the corner.

She motioned to a beautifully framed plaque on the wall. It read, *'An ye harm none, do what ye will.'*

"That is the main point of Wiccan beliefs. Do what you want to, so long as it does not hurt others. For us, others includes animals, plants, and the earth."

"Sounds like good guidelines," Doug said.

Just then, Lucy's phone rang. "Hello? Oh, hi Megan......what? Really?.........Okay, sure, let me get to my office, hang on a second."

She turned to Doug, "I have to take this. I would like to talk to you longer. Can you wait for a few minutes?"

"Sure, I will be fine," Doug assured her. He wanted to talk to her too. This was the most interesting conversation he could remember having.

After Lucy headed up the narrow staircase to her office on the second floor, Doug wandered around the mysterious room. He felt very drawn to the table in the corner. It was a two tiered table covered in a dark blue cloth with tiny gold stars all over it. There were a lot of candles in many different sizes and colors, and a very old candle snuffer. There was a basket with small amber bottles in it. He picked up a bottle. It said "Lavender". Cautiously he opened the lid and smelled it. Then he smelled "Cinnamon", "Pine", and "Bergamot". He decided that they must be essential oils. There was a small knife, with a white, mother of pearl handle, and a fancy, curvy blade. There was a cup that looked like a wine glass, only is looked like it was made from silver, with a lot of symbols carved into it. There was a small, cast iron pot with a golden symbol stamped onto the front of it. Inside were some ashes, like something had been burned in it recently. Doug recognized the symbol on the front as the same symbol that Lucy had tattooed on her ankle. A pentacle.

Next to the little pot was a long, fancy feather. Maybe from a duck or turkey, Doug thought. There were many other interesting things on the table, such as a bowl of what looked like coarse salt, a small broom type object, and a long stick with a clear crystal attached to the end of it. A magic wand? Really? On the floor near the table was a large, square pillow. It looked like it was covered in some sort of dark red satin. Doug wondered if Lucy sat here when she was in this room. In the corner opposite from the table stood a huge rock, nearly 6 feet tall, Doug estimated. It was two feet wide, and looked like a cylinder shaped rock that had been cut in half. The rock must have been mainly hollow, Doug mused. The inside walls of the rock were teaming with tiny purple crystals. Doug stood directly in front of the crystals and closed his eyes. His ears were buzzing, and his chest felt heavy standing here.

"That is called a cathedral," Lucy said, startling him as she re-entered the room. "It is a giant geode from Brazil. The crystals inside are called amethyst. Then energy is really intense around it, isn't it?"

"Is that why I feel like I have a weight sitting on my chest?" Doug finally stepped away from the crystals, feeling a little dizzy.

"Yes, you are feeling the energy of the crystals. Amethyst is known for its ability to calm the mind and body. The 'weight' feeling on your chest was your energy slowing down. Sometimes when I can't sleep, I bring a pillow and blanket in here and sleep in front of it."

Doug was mystified. He had not really believed all of this crystal stuff before, but he definitely felt something in front of the cathedral. But how could that be?

"This cathedral," Lucy began, gesturing to another giant rock in the other corner, "Is full of citrine crystals. It is also from Brazil. Tina and I got these in Brazil years ago. She has their counterparts in her house. Come over here and see if you can feel the energy from this one."

Doug hesitated, wondering if this was some kind of sin. He had never been told in church to avoid rocks that had energy, but he was still feeling a little strange. Nevertheless, his curiosity got the best of him, and he walked over to the cathedral. The crystals inside were smaller than the amethysts, and golden yellow in color. He closed his eyes and took a deep breath.

After a minute, Doug stepped back and smiled. "Joy. I felt joy standing here, like I did not have a care in the world."

"Yes, joy is a great effect of citrine. Citrine also attracts abundance, helps clear the mind of confusion and cloudy thoughts, and dispels fear and anxiety." Lucy went on, "This is where I lay my kids down to sleep if they have been having nightmares. I also help them with their homework here when they are having a hard time concentrating or learning a new subject."

Lucy was surprised that Doug was able to feel so much energy. He must be an open minded man to be able to stand here and do this, she mused. She realized that he had probably looked over her whole altar while she had been out of the room. With other people that might make her feel uncomfortable, but with Doug, she was glad in a way. If they were going to try to be friends, they had to be able to understand each other, after all.

ॐॐ

The next day at work Doug felt like he was in a fog, again. The strange evening he had experienced at Lucy's ran over and over in his head. The feelings around the crystals. The table covered in foreign tools and objects. The energy healing on Hope. The way Lucy made him feel. Doug wondered if she made everyone feel so welcome, so accepted.

"Hey, Doug," said Mark, his supervisor. "I saw your car at my neighbors house last night. Lucy?"

Doug's breath caught in his throat. What did Mark know about Lucy? "Oh, really? I did not know that you lived over in that area," Doug replied casually.

"Yep, right next door to Lucy, in fact. What a nice girl. She is constantly bringing over a loaf of fresh baked bread, brownies, or cookies. She is really becoming the 'mother' of the neighborhood. Last week she took the widow across the street, Sister Martin, to the doctor in Denver, just to help her out."

Doug let out his breath, relieved. "Our sons play on the same baseball team. My kids really like her. She invited us over for dinner last night. She is a great cook, isn't she?"

"Oh, yeah. And not bad to look at, huh, Doug?" Mark said, jabbing him in the ribs playfully. "I did not realize you were dating again!"

"No, no, not dating," Doug responded, his voice a little too loud. "We are just friends, that's all."

"Okay, okay, don't hurt yourself," Mark laughed. "I was just kidding!"

Yeah right, thought Doug. Why can't a single man be friends with a single woman without everyone in town assuming that they are dating?

Later that afternoon, Doug was paged with a personal call. He was surprised, since no one ever called him. "This is Doug Brown," he answered.

"Hi Doug," He recognized his mother's voice. "I was wondering about coming to watch Brian play ball. What time is his game tomorrow?"

扩搤

Lucy typed quickly on her laptop, excited that her new book was finally emerging. She had been struggling for a while now with a subject. Now that she had settled on something, the words were flowing out of her in a torrent. Good thing, she thought, since her publisher wanted a sample by next week. The title of the new book, she mused, might be "Outside of the Craft". She was focusing on helping other Wiccan and Pagan people to integrate their lifestyles and beliefs with others around them. Honestly, she didn't know why she was trying so hard to get a new book out so fast. She certainly did not need the money. Her simplistic lifestyle allowed her to save most of the money that her books had earned. She liked being able to spend a little here and there, but to also have the security that her kids would have a stay at home mom. She knew that their education and spiritual training was the most important job that she had right now.

Being a single mom meant that all of her energy and attention had to go to the kids. She was happy with her situation though, and would not have it any other way. Some of her friends thought that she was crazy when she, at twenty one years old, had announced that she wanted to have a baby. She had been dreaming about a baby boy named Luke for months, and she knew that it was time. Her first book had just been published, so money was no issue for her. The problem had been, who would be the daddy, since she was not even dating at the time. Finally, she decided that she would just get artificially inseminated, eliminating the issues associated with custody.

At first Tina was totally against it, but as the months marched by and the dreams continued, she finally realized that fate was dealing it's hand to Lucy. On Beltane, the Wiccan sabbat of fertility, she drove Lucy to the fertility clinic. Four weeks later Tina was brewing ginger tea to help with the morning sickness, and so on it went. She and two others from her Coven even took some midwife training classes. When Lucy went into labor, they set up an altar around her in the living room of Tina's Denver home. Candles, charms, incense, crystals, and flowers were a lot of what they used for their altar. They made her comfortable with pillows and a warm quilt. As Lucy's labor progressed, the women used energy healing to calm her pain. Tina encouraged Lucy to drink as much black and blue cohosh tea as she could, to speed labor. When the baby crowned, the women cast a circle around her, then surrounded her with love and light. A few big pushes later, and the baby was born. He was slimy and blue, but starting screaming and turning pink right away. Tina helped Lucy to cut the cord with an athame, a small, sharp knife witches use for magikal purposes. One of the other women took the baby to rub him down with a towel and wrap him in a blanket while Tina finished with Lucy. Soon after, the tiny baby was nestled happily in his mother's arms, nursing contentedly.

Lucy named the baby Luke, honoring her dreams of him. Later on, Tina told Lucy, "Of all of the magic I have witnessed, the birth of Luke has to be the most magical moment in my life." Lucy agreed whole heartedly. Two years later, her dreams returned. This time the baby was a girl, named Hope. When she told Tina, there was no arguing. It really did no good to try to argue with Lucy anyway. Again, they waited until Beltane. This time, morning sickness hit faster, and harder. Lucy and Luke ended up moving in with Tina during the pregnancy, so that she could help with Luke. When Lucy was five months along, the Doctor delivered some bad news. He told

Lucy that she was losing her amniotic fluid, and her placenta was shrinking. He told her to go home and pray for a miracle. Tina called the coven together, and the women performed a special rite on Lucy, blessing her belly, and invoking the Goddess Heket, Goddess of childbirth.

For the next week, Lucy received energy work from the women every day. When she returned to the Doctor, he did an ultra sound. He was very surprised to find that the baby was fine, the placenta was fine, and her amniotic fluid levels had returned to normal. The rest of the pregnancy proved to be uneventful. Lucy chose to deliver at home with this baby as well. Hope was born only 3 days before Luke's 3rd birthday. Lucy's labor and delivery were carried out the same way that Luke's birth was. This time, she was only in labor for two hours before Hope was born. Lucy considered Tina the grandmother to her children, and Tina was happy to assume the role.

ॐ☙

"Hurry mom, I don't want to be late for my game," Luke called, pounding on Lucy's office door.

Lucy sighed. She was so into her book that it was hard to leave. She told the kids to meet her in the car and shut down her laptop. On the way to the game, she could not help but wonder if Doug would be there. When they arrived, she scanned the crowd, but no Doug. Brian was warming up in the field, and Emily was already sitting in the bleachers. She and Hope walked over to the bleachers and sat down.

"Hi Emily," said Hope.

"Hope!" Emily squealed, giving her a hug. The two girls started laughing and talking, catching up on the events of the last two days.

Lucy smiled. It was so nice to see Hope with a friend. Just then, an older woman with white hair approached them.

"Grandma!" Emily sailed off of the bench into the woman's arms. "What are you doing here?"

"I came to see Brian play ball, silly. Can I sit with you?"

"Sure, grandma, come on!" Emily folded out the blanket she and Hope were sharing for her grandmother to sit on.

Lucy was surprised to see Emily's grandmother there, since no one had been to see Brian play all year. She had to be Doug's mother, she thought. She has the same deep blue eyes as Doug and Emily. This is really awkward, Lucy thought. I wonder if I should introduce myself. Then again, what would I say? Doug probably has not said a word about me to his mother. After all, they were just friends, right?

A few minutes after the game started, Emily started to shriek and jumped up from the bench, clutching her left hand. "A bee! A bee stung me," she cried. Her grandmother reached for her, but she was already in Lucy's arms.

Lucy rocked Emily for a moment, stroking her hair. Then she opened up her purse. She flicked the stinger out with the side of her driver's license. "It really hurts," Emily sobbed. Lucy pulled out a small amber bottle, opened the lid, and dabbed a little of the contents onto the sting. Then she placed her hand directly above the sting and sent healing energy down through it.

"Wow," Emily said, a minute later, drying her tears. "It doesn't hurt anymore. Thanks Lucy!"

Lucy realized that Emily's grandmother was staring at her. She looked up and met her gaze. "So, you are Lucy! Doug has told me so much about you." She extended her hand to Lucy. "I am Cheryl Brown, Doug's mother."

"It is so nice to meet to you," Lucy said, her head spinning. What had Doug told his mother about her, anyway?

"That is amazing, what you just did for Emily. What was in the bottle?"

"Oh, just an essential oil blend. It has lavender, sage, and tea tree." Lucy hoped that she had not noticed the energy work. "I keep a bottle in my purse for stings, bites, and sunburns."

"Wow, I need some that," said Cheryl. "I have been getting eaten by the mosquitoes in my garden this year."

"Oh, you garden? I would love to ask you some questions some time. I love to garden too, but the climate and conditions are a little different here than I am used to. I could use some good advice." Lucy was happy to be able to make a connection with Cheryl.

"Sure, anytime. I am retired, so I am home most of the time. You are welcome to come over and see my garden. Then I can answer your questions."

The two women chatted for most of the game. Cheryl asked Lucy what she did for a living. Lucy decided not to risk letting google decide anything else for her, and told Cheryl that she was a stay at home mom. During the last inning, Lucy noticed a blue Camry pull up, and Doug climb out of the car. Doug saw Lucy and waved. Then he saw Cheryl, and waved, looking puzzled.

What is going on here, he wondered. Then it hit him. His mother had called about coming to the game so that she could meet Lucy! That meddler, he fumed. She is checking up on me. "Hi mom," he said kissing her on the cheek. "What are you doing here?"

"Oh, I just wanted to see Brian play a game before the season ends." Cheryl smiled innocently. "I have just been chatting with your friend Lucy, here. She is darling!"

"Mom!" Doug exclaimed, embarrassed.

"What? She is darling, and you know it!"

Lucy blushed and looked away, stifling a giggle.

"Emily got stung by a bee, and Lucy took the pain out of it in no time flat!" Cheryl went on, "She put some oil on it from her purse, and held her hand over it for a minute, and the pain was gone. Why did you hold your hand that way Lucy, I never thought to ask?"

Doug caught Lucy's eye with a look that needed no words. Cheryl had no idea who Lucy really was. Lucy smiled calmly and said, "Oh, I was just hoping to heat up the oil so that it would absorb quicker, that's all."

Doug looked at her, relieved. What an rotten situation, he thought. Here Lucy was, just being her unique self, and he was asking her to be someone else. But she did energy work on his daughter? He was not sure that he liked that.

"Doug, I have invited Lucy over to see my garden. She loves to garden as much as I do! Would you mind bringing her over one night this week?" Cheryl maintained the sweet, innocent look on her face.

"Oh, Mom, I can't imagine that Lucy has time for that, I mean, she is really busy, and with her kids, and baseball, and work..." Doug grasped.

"Don't be silly Doug, Lucy is a stay at home mom. We have already talked about it." Cheryl turned, "How about you all come over for dinner tomorrow night?"

Lucy knew this was a bad idea, but Cheryl was so sweet, she felt bad saying no. "Well, I guess so. Will that work for you, Doug?"

Doug looked like a deer in the headlights, but managed to nod anyway.

After Cheryl left, Doug walked Lucy to her car. "Are you sure that you want to go to my parent's house? My mother is obviously up to something."

"I kind of guessed that," Lucy smiled. "But yes, I would like to. I actually have some real gardening questions for your mom. Unless you would rather that we did not go."

"No, no, I want you to go! I mean, if you want to, that is." Nice, Doug, he thought. Make a fool of yourself acting so over eager.

"It is a date then, well, I mean, not a date, but....oh, you know what I mean." Lucy was equally flustered.

"I will pick you and the kids up at 6:00 then." Doug started to walk away, then turned around, "Oh, and Lucy, thanks for helping Emily when she got stung, but no more energy work on my kids, okay?"

"Oh, okay," Lucy said, trying to keep the hurt look off of her face. Why did she have to do that anyway? The oil would have done the job by itself, but her healing instincts had kicked in. Now Doug probably thought that she was trying to push her beliefs off on his kids. No more energy work around Doug, period, she decided.

chapter 5

DOUG WAS RIGHT on time the next evening. When he pulled up, Lucy and her kids were rocking on the porch swing. When Lucy stood and descended the stairs, Doug was taken in, again, at her beauty. She was wearing a long yellow sun dress with a thin white sweater over it. Her hair was pulled back into a long, shiny ponytail, with some tiny white wildflowers nestled in it. Doug hurried out to get the door for her. For some reason, Lucy thought that Doug opening her door was really funny.

"Wow, I don't think anyone has ever done that for me before," she commented through her giggles.

"That is because you have never ridden with me," he said with a wink.

"Well, I am darling, you know," Lucy teased.

"Please, don't remind me," Doug groaned. "I can't believe my mom is turning into such a meddler."

"Alright kids, you guys are going to have to squish a little bit. Hope, Emily, can you two share a seat?" I am going to need a bigger car if this 'friendship' keeps up, Doug thought.

By the time they arrived at his parents' house, Doug's stomach was doing flip flops. What if something happens that exposes Lucy to them? How would they react? How would he react?

By that time, Lucy had already gotten out of the car, without his help, and his mom was coming down the sidewalk, his dad, right behind her. "Doug," she hissed into the car, "You should have gotten the door for her!" Doug sighed and got out.

"Hi mom, hi dad," he greeted his parents warily.

"Lucy, you already know my mom, this is my dad, Bob."

Lucy hugged Cheryl like and old friend, then grasped Bob's out-stretched hand. "Thanks to both of you for having us."

"Oh, please, don't mention it. It isn't very often that our son, here, comes over," Bob said, gesturing to Doug.

Once inside, Lucy and Doug helped Cheryl by making a green salad, then they all sat down to feast on spaghetti, garlic bread, and salad. Lucy was glad to see that her kids were using their best manners. After the meal, Brian took all of the kids outside to play on the tire swing.

"So, Lucy," Bob said, "What brings you to Rocky Point? Our pastor says that you have only lived here for a few months."

"Dad!" Doug exclaimed, mortified. "Please don't tell me you have been asking all around town about Lucy!"

Lucy laughed. "It's okay Doug, after all it is a small town. I came to Rocky Point because Denver was getting too big for my kids. I wanted to raise them somewhere that they could play outside all day without fears of crime. I also love to garden and spend time outside, and needed more space for my chickens. I bought my house because of the beautiful lot that it is on. The great old house was just an added perk."

"Well, we sure are happy to have you. My fishing buddy Jim said that you brought over some cream for his poison ivy last week that cleared it right up, plus you helped old Sister Lewis plant her garden. Seems that your neighbors can't say enough good about you, Lucy."

Lucy blushed, "Well, I try hard to be neighborly. I believe that we were all put on this planet to take good care of each other."

"What a beautiful sentiment, Lucy," said Cheryl. "If only more people had that philosophy, our world be a much happier place."

"I agree," said Doug. He was amazed at how easily Lucy conversed with his parents. She was 'charming the pants off of them', as his dad would say.

჻჻

When Doug took Lucy and the kids home at the end of the night, she turned a movie on for the kids to watch, and they sat out on the porch swing, talking. Lucy turned to him and said, "So, how did I do?"

"Great!" Too great, Doug thought. Now what am I supposed to do? My family is going to be convinced that I should date, probably even marry Lucy.

"Oh, good. I was so worried that I would embarrass you."

"Seriously? How could you ever embarrass me? I was so embarrassed by them! I can't believe that they have been out digging up information!"

Lucy laughed. "They just love you, Doug, that's all. It is a parent's job to want to see their children happy."

They sat together in comfortable silence for a time, enjoying the warm summer evening, listening to the crickets sing. Doug was thinking that he was getting more and more attached to Lucy by the day. He really did not care what her religious views were. She was quickly becoming his whole world.

Lucy was thinking along the same lines. She did not mind that Doug was Christian. He was a great guy, good to his kids, funny, and good looking. How could all of that be so wrong?

When Doug stretched his arm across the back of the swing, Lucy leaned into his chest and snuggled comfortably against him. This feels so right, Doug thought. I could stay like this forever.

"Doug, are you awake?"

"Hmmm?" Doug muttered, trying to get his bearings.

"We must have fallen asleep out here," said Lucy, shivering. "I just woke up and it is after midnight."

Lucy was still laying her head on Doug's chest. When she shivered, he wrapped his arms more tightly around her.

"I guess that I should get up and get my kids home, then." Said Doug sleepily, not moving.

"Yeah," said Lucy. "I should go get my kids up to their bedrooms." But she did not move either.

They sat on the swing in comfortable silence for a few minutes. Finally, Lucy said quietly, "Doug, can I ask you a question?"

"Sure, anything."

"I know that I shouldn't have done energy work on Emily the other day, but it is just natural for me to do it. You seemed a little angry about it, and I was just wondering why?"

"Hmm," Doug mused, why was he mad about that, anyway? "To tell you the truth, I can't even remember." Right now, with Lucy curled up in his arms, all he could think about was how good it felt to be there with her.

"I just want you to know that I really do live my coven's creed to harm none. I would never do anything to hurt you or your children. Ever."

"I could never imagine you harming anyone, Lucy. I do have a question for you, though." Doug swallowed, mustering up his courage. "How is this friend thing working out for you?"

"Well," Lucy admitted, "To be totally honest with you, not very well."

"What?" Doug was stunned. He thought things were going extremely well. Lucy and her children were starting to feel like an important part of his life.

"There is so much about you that I don't know yet," Lucy began, "but there is one thing that I know for sure. I am not able to be just friends. I need more from you, from us. I know that it goes against our belief systems to want to be together, and I have tried really hard to keep you only as a friend, but I just can't do it."

Doug smiled in the darkness. He knew that what he was going to say next would change his life forever. He also knew that he would somehow have to reconcile the rest of his life with this decision. "Lucy, I am so glad that you said that. I love being your friend, too, but this is not going to work out on my end either. I think about you all day long. When I see you, my stomach does a flip. I just can't see my life without you in it. I don't really care if you are Pagan or Wiccan, or whatever. You are the most amazing person that I have ever met."

By this time, Lucy had turned to face him. When his lips met hers, she felt a surge of electricity jolt through her body. He kissed her so softly. She was amazed by the feeling of being in his arms. There was something so real, so pure about that moment. Lucy knew then, that there was no turning back.

Lucy and Doug stayed on the swing, talking, until dawn. They decided that the best plan was to keep to themselves for the most part. There was no reason to go looking for trouble, right? Doug had suggested. Lucy agreed. After all, their relationship was no one else's business. Except, of course, for their kids.

"There is something that I need to make very clear," Doug told her. "I have no problem with you being Wiccan. At first I was scared, because I was uneducated. Now that I understand your way of life, I realize that there is nothing wrong with it. You are loving and accepting. You take excellent care of those around you. To me, that is the most important thing in the world. So, when I suggest that we keep your religion to ourselves, I want you to know that it is not because I am ashamed of you. I am just concerned that this small Christian town will not accept you, and that could make life hard for you and your kids."

"That means a lot to me," Lucy said. "I am not ashamed of my religion. In fact, I am very proud of it. I share a very rich and diverse history with others who have gone down this path. I have been quiet about it for my kids sake, though. It was hard enough for them to switch schools, without kids being afraid of them or something."

"Sure, I can understand that."

"Doug, I do have a concern, though."

"What is it, Lucy?" Doug asked, kissing her hair. "Whatever it is, we can work it out."

"At some point, someone in this small town will figure it out. Believe it or not, I am pretty famous in the New Age world. I go on book signing tours and do an occasional interview on television. Besides, it only took you one evening to find me online."

"Yeah, so? I am not ashamed of you," Doug declared emphatically. "Or of us."

"I know, it is just that I don't want life to get hard for you, that's all." Lucy couldn't stand the thought of Doug or his kids having any trouble because of her.

"Tell you what, let's just cross that bridge when we come to it," Doug said, trying to reassure her. "After all, we might be able to fly under the radar for a long time, right?"

֍֍

When the sun was cresting the sky, Doug said, "You know what, I think that I am going to do something that I have not done for three years." With that, he pulled out his cell phone, and dialed.

"Hi. Mark? Doug Brown here. I just wanted to let you know that something has come up, and I need to take a personal day off of work today.......No, no, everyone is fine, I just have a few things that I need to take care of......Sure, sure, I will see you tomorrow." He snapped his phone shut.

"I think that we have some sleeping kids in there that deserve a few answers, don't you?"

After a big breakfast of crepes with strawberries and yogurt, Doug turned to Lucy's kids. "I have a question that I need to ask you guys, okay?"

Luke and Hope looked expectantly back at him across the big wooden table. "I have asked your mom if she will date me, and she said yes. I just wanted to make sure that is okay with you two."

Hope let out a high pitched shriek and grabbed Emily. The two little girls embraced, shrieking, laughing, and dancing across the kitchen. "This is perfect," Hope told Emily. "Now we can play together all the time!"

Luke shrugged and said, "Sure, fine with me."

Lucy took Brian and Emily both by the hand. "I want to make sure this is okay with both of you, as well. Emily, you are obviously fine with it."

Emily hugged Lucy tightly, exclaiming, "Oh, I have been hoping that my daddy would date you Lucy!"

Brian, on the other hand, looked miserable. "Are you going to be my mom now? Because I already have a mom!" With that, he buried his head in his hands and sobbed.

"Oh, Brian!" Doug started towards him, but Lucy held up her hand.

Lucy knelt and held Brian as great sobs racked his body. She whispered in his ear, "Brian, I know how much you love your mom, and that you probably miss her every day. I want to promise you that I will not do anything to try to take her place. I will be your friend, and I will do anything that you ask me to do. But I will not ever, ever try to make you forget your mom." Finally, Brian pulled away from her and dried his red eyes.

He held out his hand to Lucy, and said, "It is a deal," as they shook hands.

After breakfast, Doug and his kids went home to shower and change, with plans to pick Lucy and the kids up later to go to Denver. Lucy need to get her car serviced and run a few errands. Doug volunteered to go with her so that she could leave her car with the mechanic for a few days.

❧⚬❦

"Mom," Hope wailed from the backseat, "I am starving! When are we going to eat?"

"Me too," Luke chimed in. "I am so hungry I could eat a house!"

Lucy noticed a little roadside diner coming up, so she turned on her blinker and pulled in. Doug pulled in behind her and climbed out.

"Good idea, my kids think that they are starving to death!" Doug told her. "Besides, my brothers love this place. They say that the fresh cut fries are amazing."

After the waitress seated them, Lucy took Hope and Emily to the bathroom. Doug gave the boys a few quarters to play the arcade games in the corner. Doug was looking out the window, thinking about the amazing turns his life had taken the last few weeks. Outside he noticed a familiar truck pull up and park. There was a logo on the side, 'B&D Landscaping'. Two couples climbed out and headed for the door, stopping briefly to look at his car, parked near the door. Doug groaned. I should have known my brothers would show up here, he thought!

"It can't be Doug's car," he heard David's voice boom. "Doug never, ever misses work. Unless he has had car trouble?"

"Isn't that him in that booth, over there?" Liz pointed in Doug's direction.

Doug was slouching down, trying to be invisible.

"Hi Doug," Brandon said, tapping him on the shoulder.

"Uh, oh, hi guys." Dang it, Doug thought. Now what?

"Are you having car trouble?" David asked him.

"No, why?" Doug knew that Lucy would be out the bathroom any minute now.

"I don't know, it is just odd seeing you here. Why aren't you at work?" David sounded suspicious.

Doug's heart was racing, palms sweating, breathing shallow. He felt like a deer in the headlights. "I just, uh, well......um, can't a guy take a day off here and there? I deserve a break!"

"Okay, okay, calm down," Brandon laughed. "We were just surprised to see you here, that's all."

You think you are surprised now, Doug thought. Just like they had been cued, Lucy and the girls emerged from the bathroom. Emily recognized her aunts and uncles and ran to them, squealing.

"Uncle David, Uncle Brandon, Aunt Liz, Aunt Nicole!" She went around, hugging them all.

Lucy took her seat in the booth across from a miserable looking Doug. Four adults were staring at her, their mouths agape. Doug was here with a woman?

"Hi," She said, smiling, "I am Lucy. You must be Doug's brothers, the landscapers, right?"

With that, Doug seemed to recover his composure. "Lucy, I would like you to meet my brothers, Brandon and David, and their wives, Nicole and Liz."

Lucy stood and shook each of their hands. "Are you here for lunch? You really should join us! I'm sure that we can pull another table over."

"Oh, no, there isn't really enough room here," Doug said, willing to try anything to get rid of his nosy siblings.

"Oh, don't be silly Doug," Brandon smiled innocently, sliding and extra table effortlessly over to them. "We can make it work."

"Great," Doug said, forcing a smile. Lucy has no idea what she is in for here, he thought. These four will ask her a thousand questions.

After everyone was seated and had ordered, Lucy broke the ice. "You mother told me all about your landscape business. I was planning on calling about some trees."

"Really, what do you need?" asked David, always happy to pick up a new client.

"I want some fast growing trees to plant around the front of my property to provide some privacy from the street," Lucy responded.

With that, David and Brandon started talking about different tree options, the best time to plant, and so on. Wow, thought Doug. Lucy is good at keeping them talking about themselves!

After the food came, Liz said, "Alright. Enough work talk. I have a million questions for you, Lucy!" Liz was amazed at how relaxed and laid back Lucy was. She effortlessly helped her kids with their lunches, ate hers, and carried on a conversation.

Lucy smiled at her. "Sure Liz, what do you want to know?"

"Well, first of all, that is such a beautiful necklace. What is it?" Lucy had a large blue stone hanging from her neck, the top of it wrapped in copper wire.

"This is a crystal called Celestite. My adoptive mother is a geologist. She brought this back from Madagascar recently." Lucy refrained from mentioning that Celestite has many metaphysical properties, such as being calming, balancing, and creating harmony.

"Wow," said Nicole. "It is really pretty."

"Thanks!"

"So, Lucy," began Brandon, "Where are you from?"

"I was born in California, but I lived in Denver from the time I was ten until a few months ago."

"Really, so what brought you to Rocky Point?" Liz asked, her chin resting on her palm.

"I wanted my kids to slow down a little bit. Also, I love to garden, keep chickens, that sort of thing. The city was getting too big for us." Lucy looked over at Doug and smiled reassuringly. He looked like he was finally starting to relax.

"That's great," chimed in Nicole. "Rocky Point is a wonderful place to raise kids, that is for sure."

"What do you do for a living, Lucy?" Brandon asked.

"I am mostly a stay at home mom," replied Lucy. "I write here and there, but that is about it."

"You write? That is so interesting. What do you write about?" Brandon inquired.

"Oh, you know, herbs, gardening, stuff like that," Lucy replied, without missing a beat.

"You know, Lucy, we had better be going if we are going to get your car to the shop," Doug cut in, realizing that it was time for this interview to be over.

"Well, Lucy, it was great to meet you," Liz said, as they walked to the parking lot.

"Yeah, I hope you will join us on Sunday for dinner at Bob and Cheryl's" added Nicole.

∾∾

When Lucy and Doug pulled into the auto repair shop in Denver, Doug wondered if he should go in with her. "Lucy, do you want me to come in with you and help explain what your car needs?"

"Well, okay, if you want to," Lucy said, puzzled. Why would I need help explaining what my car needs?

As they walked in the door, Doug made a note of the sign above him. 'Mitchy and Les Auto Repair'.

When they walked into the shop, a heavy set woman with short, spiky hair looked up over the hood of a Volvo. She looked like she must be in her 50's.

"Hey, if it isn't Lucy! Good to see you, girl!" She hurried over to Lucy, wiping her hands on a rag that she had pulled from the back pocket of her blue coveralls.

"Hi, Mitchy," Lucy smiled, embracing her.

"Les, get out here and see what the cat dragged in!" Mitchy yelled towards the office.

A taller, thin woman with long blonde hair in a braid hurried out of the office to see what was going on. "Well, Lucy!" She exclaimed, hurrying over to embrace her. "Are you bringing your old bomb in for some work?"

Lucy laughed, "Yeah, it is time for a good tune up. And how could you say that about my car? You are the one who sold it to me!"

"Yeah, ten years ago. I thought that by now you would have upgraded," countered Les.

"No way. I love my car." Lucy said, "Besides, why replace it when there is nothing wrong with it?"

"True, true." Agreed Mitchy.

"This is my friend Doug, by the way," Lucy introduced. "Doug, these are my friends, Les and Mitchy. They have been keeping me on the road since I started driving."

Both Les and Mitchy shook Doug's hand firmly. Doug was polite, but very surprised. He had never been in a repair shop owned by women before.

In fact, the thought of female mechanics had never crossed his mind. One thing he had learned from his experiences with Lucy so far, though, was that she knew a lot more about the world than he did.

"Great shop you've got here," he complimented. "I am going to need a tune up in a month or so. Do you suppose you could get me in?"

Lucy beamed. "Oh, Doug, that would be so great. You can really trust these two. They are always honest and ethical."

"Sure, Doug," said Mitchy. "Be happy to."

After they left the shop, Lucy and her kids piled in with Doug and his kids. "They seem nice." Doug commented.

"They really are. When they first opened, they got a lot of resistance. People were not sure what to think about this shop owned and operated by lesbian women. It took them a while to build up a clientele, but now they stay really busy."

Doug glanced over at her in surprise. "Lesbian women? I did not realize that."

"Well don't get weirded out now," Lucy laughed. "They are wonderful. They have always been so good to me."

"So, are they, uh, together, or what?"

"They are partners, yes. They have been together for over twenty five years."

Wow, Doug thought, feeling a little naive. "That is impressive. I guess I did not realize that those kind of people had long term relationships."

Lucy stared at him. "Those 'kind' of people? Doug, do you have a problem with gay people?"

"No, I don't think so. I just don't know any gay people, that's all."

"Yes, you do," Lucy replied. "There must be gays where you work. They may not be comfortable telling people at work. That kind of thing can get people fired if their boss is homophobic."

"No way!" Doug exclaimed. "Wouldn't that be against the law?"

"Technically, yes. But the boss will just find some other reason to get rid of them if they have a problem with their orientation."

"I had no idea." Man, thought Doug. Had he been living in a bubble his whole life?

Lucy was smiling to herself about this conversation. Doug was so cute, so sheltered. Somehow, though, he managed to be really accepting of other people. That made him a gem in Lucy's opinion.

chapter 6

THE NEXT DAY at work, Mark cornered Doug by the copy machine. "Do you know what I saw yesterday, on my way to work?"

"What?" Doug asked, wondering what Mark was up to.

"I saw your car parked at my neighbor's house, just a few minutes after you called in for the day." Mark was smiling, his eyes twinkling. "Can you believe that?"

Dang, I completely forgot about Mark living by Lucy, thought Doug. "Yeah, well, I was just helping her with some yard work, that's all." Doug shifted uncomfortably.

"At 6:45 in the morning? Yeah, right. What is the real scoop?" Mark was really enjoying watching Doug squirm.

"Okay, listen, I am dating Lucy," Doug confessed. "We are hoping to keep our relationship private for awhile, though. Do you suppose you could keep this under your hat for me?"

"Oh, sure. No problem Doug. You can count on me!" Mark clapped him on the shoulder and winked at him.

Doug headed back to his desk, vowing to be more careful in the future. After lunch, a guy Doug thought was named Brad stuck his head in the office door.

"So, is it true? I am freaking out!"

"Is what true?" Doug was taken off guard by the sudden intrusion.

"You, dating Lucy Meriweather? I just love her. My girlfriend and I have seen her speak several times. She is just amazing."

"Oh, you have? Um, well yes. I guess we are dating. I didn't realize anyone in this office would know her."

"Seriously? Doug, the woman is a legend in Denver. The whole office is buzzing about it. Listen, my girlfriend's birthday is coming up. If I bring you a book, do you think you could ask Lucy to sign it? If she has time, I mean. It would mean a lot to both of us."

"Um, I guess so. I mean, I can ask her." Doug shook his head in amazement as Brad closed his office door. Who knew that he was dating a celebrity? How is it that so many people in my office know Lucy's work, he wondered. I always though that people here were a lot like me. He started thinking about his conversation with Lucy about gay people. She said that he had gay people in his office, he just didn't know it. Now he was realizing that there were all kinds of people in his office with all kinds of beliefs.

Suddenly, Doug was looking at his coworkers in a new light. They were all wonderful people that he respected. He had always loved this firm. When his wife died, they all rallied around him for months. If he needed to miss work when one of his kids was sick, they were always understanding. They were good people, he knew. Gay, straight, Christian, pagan, atheist, whatever. It didn't matter to him anymore.

છ~જ

The rest of the week went by in a flurry. During the day, Lucy was busy weeding her garden, planting flowers, and working on her book. Luke and Hope were having a blast riding their bikes, exploring the woods behind their house, and playing with Emily and Brian in the evenings.

On Thursday after work, Doug and the kids came over for dinner. After they ate, Lucy asked Doug for some help.

"I am hosting the Summer Solstice with my coven this year, and I could use some help gathering wood. The kids and I have already made a big fire pit way out at the end of the property. Would you mind helping me with the chainsaw?"

"Sure," Doug replied, "But what is this Solstice thing?"

"The Summer Solstice, or Litha, as it is often called, is the longest day of the year. It is usually on June 21st, which is Saturday this year."

"Why is the longest day of the year so exciting?" Doug asked, walking with her out to the shed.

"Wiccans celebrate eight Sabbats throughout the year. The first is Samhain, which is our New Year's Eve. Litha is the sixth Sabbat. It is the end of the half year reign of the Oak King, and the beginning the reign on the Holly King. This ends the waxing of the year, and begins the waning."

Doug looked at her, his head cocked to one side. "I'm listening."

"Fire is a very important part of the Litha. The ancients would have huge bonfires on the tops of hills to assist the sun in changing its course. We have a fire on Litha now to honor it as one of the basic five elements."

"I see," said Doug picking up the chainsaw. "So what are the other four elements?"

"Water, air, earth, and ether, or spirit." Lucy said, as she walked with Doug out to the woods bordering her property.

They selected a few fallen trees and worked together to cut them into manageable sizes and hauled the wood to the fire pit. Lucy instructed Doug to cut two logs into four foot lengths that they buried one foot deep, two feet apart near the fire pit, facing east. Then they nailed a board over the top of it to form a high table.

"What is this for?" Doug asked.

"An alter. The High Priestess will use this space during our ceremony."

Lucy sat down in the grass next to the alter, and Doug joined her. "She will be in charge of part of the ceremony, and I will be in charge of part of it. Since I am the host, it is my honor to plan and carry out some sort of ritual with the group."

"Wow, so this is really a lot more than just some friends getting together for a bonfire, isn't it?"

"Oh, yeah. The sabbats are very important to us. It is like you going to church on Sunday. It is the time that you learn your religion, talk to your leaders, and pray right?"

"Right."

"Well, this is like our church service, I guess you could say. Make no mistake, we will have plenty of time for fun, too. We will stay up most of the night visiting and reconnecting."

"But you said that there are eight sabbats, right?" Doug clarified. "That means that you only meet for services eight times per year. Most Christian churches meet at least once a week. That is a big difference. How do the people in your coven keep their faith strong when they meet so rarely?"

"We do meet for other reasons too, like initiations and things like that. It seems to me that you are hitting on one of the biggest differences between your religion and mine, though. In Wicca, everyone is on their own sacred path. It is all very individual. There is no big book like the bible that is full of our rules and dogma."

"Really?"

"Nope. No one is ever going to tell you what you have to believe, and what you can't believe. Some Wiccans really only practice their craft when they come to the Sabbats, and some others practice their craft every day. There are lots of practicing Wiccans who don't even have a coven, and practice completely on their own. Any way is fine. It is not up to me, or the High Priestess, or anyone else to judge how involved someone is."

"But how do you end up with any beliefs, then?" Doug asked. "I feel like I need someone who is more spiritual than I am to tell me what is what. I have never really been able to do that on my own. The leaders in my church have a deeper connection to God than I do, so I rely on their counsel."

"Well, we learn how to listen to our own intuition. I, personally, receive a lot of inspiration when I meditate and when I write."

"But how do you know that the inspiration you receive is right?"

"Because, Doug. I am a divine being, therefore, anything that comes from me is divine." Lucy laughed at the look on Doug's face. "I know, that sounds easier than it is, huh?"

"Well, yeah." Doug was awed by Lucy's confidence. He was not sure if he had ever really had any inspiration. And a divine being? Lucy, no doubt, was a divine being, in Doug's opinion. But Doug wasn't so sure about himself.

๑๑

Saturday was a busy day for Lucy. Doug and the kids came over first thing in the morning to help out. They had both agreed that he would go home before the guests started coming, however. Neither of them were quite ready to announce their relationship. There was food to prepare, guest beds to make up, and a lawn to mow.

By the end of the morning, most of the jobs were done. Lucy and Doug were standing in the kitchen icing the sheet cakes that Lucy had baked earlier that morning.

"Wow, Doug, you are pretty good at cake decorating." Lucy smiled innocently, wiping yellow frosting across Doug's cheek.

"Oh, you are gonna pay for that one," Doug grabbed Lucy around the waist as she tried to run, and spread pink frosting across her forehead.

A frenzy of laughing, shrieking, and frosting smearing ensued. Lucy and Doug were chasing each other around the kitchen with spatulas, landing a blow of frosting where ever they could.

అశ్ఁ

"Wow, Lucy wasn't kidding. This is a cool old house," commented Megan from the back seat of Tina's blazer, as they pulled into the driveway. "I love the energy here."

"I know what you mean," Tina replied, putting the car in park and shutting off the ignition. "This is a special place. No wonder she was willing to move clear out here."

"Well," Amber chimed in, "Should we surprise Lucy? We are at least two hours early. She will be so glad that we came early to help!"

The sounds of screaming were coming from the open window in the living room as the three women walked up the stone steps. Tina threw the door open and ran towards the noise, with Megan and Amber right behind her. She reached the kitchen just in time to see Lucy hurl a handful of green frosting across the room and hit a tall blond man in the face with it.

"Take that," Lucy yelled triumphantly.

"Uh, Lucy," Doug gestured, pointing at the strangers who had just raced into the kitchen.

Lucy turned, very surprised to see Tina, Megan and Amber staring at her. "Oh, hi guys. You are early!"

"We came early to see if we could help out." Amber explained, turning her head to one side, surveying the huge mess in the kitchen. "Everyone else will be here at 5:00. Sounds like there will be about forty of us. A few people are bringing their kids, and there are a couple of teenagers coming to baby sit so that all of the adults can stay outside with the group."

"That's great," said Lucy. "We were just frosting cakes for tonight." Doug was already at her side with a dish towel trying to free a big glob of yellow frosting from the top of her head.

"Really?" Asked Tina, giggling. "I should share my recipe with you. It is a lot cleaner than this."

With that, everyone laughed. Doug was not sure what to say, or do. He felt bad that Lucy had so much frosting matted to her beautiful long hair. She had started it though, he reasoned.

"Hi," he said, holding out his hand to Tina. "I am Doug."

"Oh," Tina's green eyes widened. "So you are Doug. Well it is very nice to meet you!" She clasped his hand in both of hers warmly.

Doug smiled at Tina. So, this is the high priestess? She was in her late fifties, had long, wavy silver hair, and a very pleasant face. Doug was taken in by her kind smile.

"Likewise," Doug replied.

"I am Megan, and this is Amber," Megan cut in. "Lucy did not mention that you were so cute!"

"Megan!" Lucy shrieked, holding up a frosting covered spatula as a warning.

"What? He is!" Megan laughed, ducking.

Doug was hoping to be home before the guests started to arrive, but he knew he could not just duck out now, with Lucy standing there covered in frosting. "Tell you what Lucy, why don't you go get cleaned up, and I will take care of the kitchen."

"Oh, Doug, you are wonderful!" She hugged him, making the mess on the two of them even worse. Then she turned to her guests, "Why don't you three give yourselves a tour of the house, and I will be back down in a few minutes."

After Doug had scrubbed the kitchen and finished the cakes, he headed into the bathroom to clean himself up. He laughed out loud when he saw how much frosting he had in his eyebrows. Lucy is so much fun to be around, he thought.

After he finished washing up, he noticed that Lucy's friends were unloading their car, so we went out to help.

"What can I do to help out?" He asked Tina.

"Here," Megan handed him a box that clanged with the sound of glass bottles banging against each other. "Can you take these in and put them in the fridge?"

Doug opened the box when he got to the fridge. There was twelve bottles of wine inside. As he took each bottle from the box, he examined them curiously. They ranged from being yellowish in color, to being dark jewel tones of purple and red. The labels were the most interesting, though. "Old Crone Winery" was printed across the top, then a fantastic picture of the Rocky Mountains. Across the bottle, the type of wine was listed, things like Perfectly Plum, Peachy Keen, Soulful Strawberry, and Harmony Huckleberry.

"Pretty cool labels, huh?" Tina placed a second case of wine on the floor.

"Yeah, they are. Where is 'Old Crone Winery'?"

"My basement. I have made wine for years as a hobby. I love to bring it to get togethers like this to share."

"Wow," said Doug. "I had no idea that people could make their own wine at home. What does 'Old Crone' mean?"

"Well, basically it means 'Old Lady'. The crone is the third aspect of the Goddess. The first aspect is the Maiden, then the Mother, then Crone. I am getting older, so I am now considered a Crone. In Wicca that is a good thing, though. The crone is thought to be full of wisdom, magic and power."

"Hmm, that sounds like a great title to have," Doug commented. "Is that why you are the High Priestess?"

"No, I am the High Priestess because my mother was the high priestess before me, and her mother before her. Not all covens operate on the Right of Succession, but ours does. It is a tremendous honor for me to serve the coven."

"How old were you when you became High Priestess, if you don't mind me asking?" Doug did not want to seem nosy, but he was fascinated by Tina.

"I was too young, only thirty two. My mother died in a terrible car accident, and the coven turned to me to take over. It was a very difficult time for me."

"I am sure it was," Doug sympathized.

"My mother had trained me well in the traditions, but I had not really done any ceremonies or rituals in public before. If it had not been for the Crones in the coven, I probably would not have made it through the first year."

Tina had turned to look out the window. "Two years later, fate brought me a new challenge. A young mother from California came to Denver, and contacted me. She said that she was new in town and looking for a coven. I invited her over to my house to talk. When she arrived, she had a beautiful little ten year old daughter with her. In the course of talking with her, I discovered that she had fled California because of her abusive husband. She had no money, car, or anything."

"Wow, that is so sad," Doug said, shaking his head.

"I was not really sure what to do, but I knew what my mother would have done. I invited them to stay with me until she was on her feet. They moved into one of the spare bedrooms. After six months of trying to find work, she decided that she was going to have to go back to California and try to figure things out. She asked me if I could keep her daughter with me for a few more weeks, and said she would send for her as soon as possible. I agreed, of course."

"She must have really trusted you to leave her daughter like that."

"Yeah, she did. But then a few weeks turned into a few months, that turned into a few years. I never heard from her again, yet she left with me the most precious gift in the world."

"Lucy." Doug was so touched by this story, by this genuine, wonderful woman.

"Lucy," Tina repeated. "Even at ten she had something so special about her. She has taught me more about life and love than any other person I have ever met. Raising her was a joy."

"She is amazing," Doug agreed.

"So, if you don't mind me asking, are you two dating now?"

"We are. We had been hoping to keep it a secret a little longer. We have been really enjoying the bliss of being together, and have been a little worried about how our community would react if they discovered Lucy was a witch," Doug explained. "It makes me feel bad though, like I am hiding some filthy secret, only to me, it is not bad. I just don't ever want Lucy to think that I am ashamed of her."

Tina pondered this for a moment. "I can see why you are worried, I suppose. How strong will your town's reaction be, do you think?"

"It is anyone's guess," Doug admitted. "I really expect though, that it will be ugly for a while. People in this town are nearly all the same religion. I think that it makes it hard for outsiders, no matter who they are."

"I am sure that is true," Tina agreed.

"Pagans in general are completely misunderstood, so people may jump to some crazy conclusions. These are good people, though, so I am really hoping that once they figure out that Lucy is not worshiping the devil or something silly like that, things will settle down."

"Sure, it will. Things will all come out in the wash, they always do," Tina reassured him. "One question, though. You are a part of this community, and the local religion. Why didn't you shun Lucy when you learned that she was Wiccan?"

"Well, I am ashamed to say that I did, for a little while," Doug admitted. "But I just couldn't stay away. There is something so real, so pure about Lucy. I felt so connected to her the moment that I met her. I could not imagine how someone so amazing could be bad. After I starting asking questions about Wicca and doing some reading on my own, I realized that this is a beautiful religion. And, of course, there was no devil worship to be found."

"Unfortunately, it was the early Christians who started that rumor," replied Tina.

"Yeah, I know. That is not a good mark for Christians, that is for sure," Doug frowned. "Maybe that is a part of what my job will be here in Rocky Point. To help dispel rumors and mistakes."

"That is very likely, I think. Two thousand years of beliefs may not be easy to dispel however." Tina patted his arm.

"Let me ask you something, though. How will your community respond to Lucy dating a Christian? Isn't that a contradiction to your faith as well?" Doug asked.

"Well, no, actually. We believe that all people are free to do as they will, so long as they do not hurt others. The people of our coven love Lucy dearly. They are only concerned with her happiness." Tina smiled at Doug. "If you are the thing that makes her happy, then we will support her fully."

"Who will support who fully?" Lucy asked entering the kitchen to find her boyfriend and her mother sitting on the floor in front of the refrigerator, talking.

Doug looked up at her sheepishly. "Well, I was just talking to Tina about how your coven may react to you dating a rouge, dangerous Christian."

"Oh, really?" Lucy giggled. "And what did you discover?"

"That no one really cares how Christian I am, so long as I make you happy," Doug sighed, feigning regret.

"Wow, that really puts a dent in your bad boy image, doesn't it?" Lucy teased him.

"My ego has been shattered by this news, if you must know." Doug was fighting back laughter now. He stood and offered a hand up to Tina.

"Doug, it was wonderful getting to know you," she told him.

"Likewise. Thanks for listening." Doug realized that Tina had such a peaceful presence about her that he felt better about everything just by talking to her. A lot like the feeling he got from Lucy, he mused.

"Well, Lucy, I think that I am going to head home." Doug called out the back door for his kids, who had been playing outside all day with Hope and Luke.

Lucy walked him to the car. "I really appreciate everything you have done to help me out today."

"Sure, Lucy. Anytime. I hope that you have a wonderful Summer Solstice!" With that he bent over and kissed her. "I want to hear all about it tomorrow."

"Deal!" Lucy smiled and walked back to the house.

On the way home, Doug was thinking a lot about what Tina had told him. The fascinating story about Lucy's birth mother coming to town and leaving Lucy with Tina kept rolling around in his head. No wonder Lucy could relate so well to his kids, she knew how it felt to lose your mother.

ॐॐ

Lucy's afternoon was full of laughter and fun as she reunited with old friends and finished the preparations for the evening celebrations. It was so great to have so many people that she loved at her new house. Many of them pitched tents in the yard to stay over in. She set a few of them up in guest rooms. It felt so good to be around people who knew her and understood her.

At eight in the evening, the coven gathered around the wooded altar that Lucy and Doug had built. Tina had placed several items of importance on the altar. First, she picked up a small brass bell and rang it once. "The ceremony has begun!" She announced. The coven watched her quietly.

Next, Tina picked up a small silver knife, her athame. Standing behind the altar, she pointed the athame downward, and walked deosil, or clockwise, all the way around the fire pit and the gathered coven, beginning the sacred ritual of casting the circle. As she walked, her voice rang out, "I consecrate this circle to the Goddess and the God. Here they may manifest and bless us, their children!"

When she returned to the altar, she turned to face East. She raised her arms with her athame in her right hand, and declared, "This is a time that is not a time, in a place that is not a place, on a day that is not a day. We stand together at the threshold between the worlds, before the Veil of Mysteries. May those of the Old Religion protect us, that we may stay true to the path forever! By the golden rays of the sun, and the silvery light of the moon, by the light of every star in the vast and mysterious firmament, by all of these signs I do call and command you with this sacred blade. Guard us in this time and place from all unbalanced forces!"

Then Tina laid the athame on the altar, and turned to face her coven. "Join me in inviting spirits who would help us."

All the people in the circle raised their arms and said in unison, "Come, all of those who will help us this night. We welcome you within our sacred circle. We bid you to join your powers with ours, that we may create and accomplish much!"

Next Tina picked up the athame again, also a chalice of water. She touched the surface of the water with the blade and said, "May the blessings of the Goddess be upon this water, the symbol of the sacred element of Water. May it always serve as a reminder to us of the endless waters of rebirth."

Then she put the chalice of water down, and placed the tip of the blade into to a small stone bowl of salt. "The blessings of the Goddess be upon this salt, representing the sacred element of the Earth. May we always honor the earth, as it is her body in the physical world."

She scooped some of the salt out of the bowl with the tip of the blade, and placed it into the chalice of water, combining them. She swirled the water clockwise three times. Then she held the chalice high over the alter, and proclaimed, "Water and earth, both elements of birth. By touch, purify. By power, sanctify. Great Goddess, we adore you!" Again, Tina walked clockwise around the circle, sprinkling the salt water around the edge with her fingers.

When she returned to the altar, she put down the chalice and placed her blade over a small tablet of burning charcoal that had been lit earlier The charcoal was inside of a small cast iron cauldron. "May the blessings of the God be upon this charcoal, symbol of the sacred element of fire. May we always honor the sacred fire that burns brightly in all of us!"

After that, she held the blade over a small dish with powdered incense in it. "May the blessings of the God be upon this incense, symbol of the sacred element Air. May we always listen to the intuition that whispers to our souls!"

With that, Tina laid the athame back on the altar, and placed a pinch of incense on the charcoal tablet. She picked the cauldron up and held it high over the altar. "Fire and Air, elements so fair. By touch, purify. By power, sanctify. Great God, we do adore you!" Then she walked the circle again, clockwise, swinging the handle of the cauldron to disperse the smoke from the burning incense.

When she returned to the altar, she faced the coven with arms raised, and proclaimed, "Round and round, the power has bound. The circle is cast!"

"So mote it be!" Exclaimed the coven.

"It is time to call in the four directions," said Tina. "Will those who have been asked please come to the altar now?"

Four witches walked solemnly to the altar. A young man named Michael took a burning white candle from the altar, and carried it to the East of the circle, where a yellow candle was waiting for him. As he lit the candle, he called out, "Spirits of the East, all those who are ruled by the sacred Element of Air, we do summon you to witness this ritual and to guard this circle!"

When he was finished, he replaced the white candle to the altar and joined the coven. Next, a nervous looking woman who Tina recognized as a new initiate, took the white candle from the altar and walked to the South, lighting a red candle at the edge of the circle. She cleared her throat and called out, "Spirits of the South, all those who are ruled by the sacred Element of Fire, we do summon you to witness this ritual and to guard this circle!" She smiled, relieved that she had completed her assignment without error, and returned the white candle to the altar.

Next, Megan came to the altar and took the white candle. She walked to the West, lighting a blue candle at the edge of the circle. "Spirits of the West, all those who are ruled by the sacred Element of Water, we do summon you to witness this ritual and to guard this circle!"

Finally, the last witch, a balding man named Rick, took the white candle and walked to the North, and lit a green candle at the edge of the circle. "Spirits of the North, all those who are ruled by the sacred Element of Earth, we do summon you to witness this ritual, and to guard this circle!"

Lucy shivered with excitement. She always loved the circle casting ritual. It was so real, and the energy inside the circle felt electric to her tonight. It would be her turn to lead part of the summer solstice ceremony soon.

Tina turned her attention to the coven and smiled. "Welcome! I am so excited to see all of you here. I truly love the Summer Solstice sabbat. What a beautiful night we have been given for our worship. As you all know, the Summer Solstice is the longest day of the year. It was on this day that the ancients built bonfires on hilltops to worship the sun. At this time, we see the Goddess as heavily pregnant, as the crops are flourishing now, and will be ready for harvest soon. The great God, the Oak King, who serves as consort to the Goddess through the first half of the year, is defeated on this day by the Holly King, who will take over as consort to the Goddess for the rest of the year. We are reminded this time of year, that life is ever waxing, then waning, then waxing again."

Lucy looked around at the group as Tina spoke. She was taken in by the sincerity of Tina's words, and by the undivided attention that the coven was giving her. Lucy felt a deep surge of love and connection to all of those in the circle with her.

"Let us begin the Summer Solstice celebration by inviting the Nature spirits to join us!" Tina proclaimed.

Lucy stepped forward to the altar, and lit a tall green candle. She looked to the sky and called out, "We welcome the Goddess to our circle this night. To all of you Fairies, Elves, and other friendly nature spirits, welcome! The energy and magic that flows within us and within this circle is strong. We ask for your friendship, and your companionship, for we too, walk a path of magic and power."

Next, Lucy lit a tall gold candle. Again, she tilted her head skyward and called out, "We welcome the God to our circle. May his blessing come upon all who stand in this circle!"

Lucy placed her hands over the water in the chalice, and said, "Bless this water with your touch, oh Goddess and God. May this water serve as connection for us to the Hidden Well of Wisdom."

Lucy placed her index finger in the water, then touched it to her forehead, lips and heart. She knelt before the altar, and said a silent prayer to the God and Goddess, rededicating her life. She then rose, took a handful of herbs from a basket on the altar, and walked to the crackling fire. "On this Summer Solstice, I humbly ask the Goddess to give me the inspiration that I need to finish my new book, that it will serve as a bridge between faiths, and bring more people together in love and unity!" With that she threw the herbs into the fire, sealing her request.

One by one, the coven members approached the altar, anointed themselves with the blessed water, knelt before the alter in prayer, then made a request to the God or Goddess at the fire, and sealed their requests with herbs. The requests ranged from things like health, prosperity, knowledge, and love.

When all participants had taken their turn at the altar, Lucy returned to the altar and took a large silver chalice from underneath. She filled it from a carafe of wine. Using her own athame, she gently touched the tip to of the blade to the surface of the wine. "As the athame is the male, the chalice is the female, and joined as one, they bring blessings."

She raised the chalice high over her head, and in unison with the group said, "To the Goddess and the God! Merry meet, and merry part, and merry meet again!" Then Lucy took a small drink of wine from the chalice, and handed it to Tina, who drank, and passed it on. When everyone had taken a sip, Lucy poured the rest of the wine in the chalice into the earth as an offering. For the next couple of hours, the coven drank wine, ate cake, and enjoyed each others company.

Finally, Tina returned to the altar to close the circle. She started at the yellow candle of the East. As she extinguished the candle with a candle snuffer, she called out, "Spirits of the East, all of those ruled by the Element of Air, we bid you peacefully depart. Our thanks, and farewell."

She continued on, releasing the South, West, and North in the same manner. After that she returned to the altar, raised her arms, and said, "Fairies, Spirits, Elementals, and all of the invisibles, we give our thanks and our blessing. May we always work in love and harmony with one another. Blessed be!"

"Blessed be!" The coven repeated.

Tina took her athame to the eastern point of the circle, and made a cutting motion with it. "The circle is cut but the blessings remain. Merry meet, and merry part, and merry meet again! Blessed be!"

With the ending of the ritual, many people turned to embrace each other, thanking them for their presence there. The party around the bonfire went deep into the night, as old friends reconnected. Lucy was filled with love and peace. She could not help but wonder, though, what Doug was doing tonight. She was starting to miss him more and more when they were apart.

chapter 7

THE NEXT MORNING, Lucy rose early and walked out to her garden. All of her guests were still sleeping, as were her children. She sat cross legged on the grass and began her morning meditation.

On the other side of town, Doug and the kids were getting ready for church. He had been asked to say the opening prayer this morning, so they needed to be on time. When they arrived early, Pastor Jones came down and sat in the pew next to Doug.

"Good morning Doug, it is so good to see you."

"It is good to see you too, Pastor."

"I have been meaning to come by and visit. How are you and the kids getting along." Doug wondered where this was coming from.

"We are doing just fine. Why do you ask?"

"Well, to be honest with you Doug, I have been hearing rumors that you have been spending a lot of time at my neighbor's house. I just wondered if there is anything that you would like to talk to me about, that's all."

That Mark, Doug thought. This has to be his doing. "Well, yes, I have been spending a lot of time with Lucy. Our kids really like to play together."

"Sure, sure. Of course they do. But what about you and Lucy?"

"I do enjoy Lucy's company," Doug admitted. "She is a wonderful person."

"Oh, yes. The whole neighborhood loves her, that is true. Let me ask you something, though. Why haven't I seen her at church? It seems to me that someone who is so Christ-like must be religious."

"Well, she is not a part of our church, that's all." Doug was really getting uncomfortable. Did the Pastor know more that he was letting on? Also, Doug hated the idea that Lucy had to be Christian to be a good person. Why couldn't she just be considered a good person because of her good deeds?

"I see. Well, Doug, I have to tell you, I would be much more comfortable with you dating someone from our church. You never know what you are going to get if you don't." With that, Pastor Jones stood, squeezed Doug's shoulder, and headed to the pulpit.

Doug was shocked. What gave the pastor the right to tell him who he could and could not date? As he mulled over what the pastor had said, the rest of his family filed in and joined him and his kids on the pew. The organ music eventually faded, and the Pastor stood up to the pulpit, welcoming everyone to church. When he was cued, Doug stood and walked to the pulpit. He said the opening prayer, asking God to bless everyone in Rocky Point with health and happiness. He had a hard time listening to the service. His eyes drifted around the church. The chapel felt so familiar to him. He had been coming here since he was a baby. The organ pipes embedded in mahogany wood, the huge stained glass windows that let in beautiful patterns of light that danced around on the floor. It all felt so comforting to him. He had married his wife here, then held her funeral here. He had blessed both of his children here. Then there were the people. People who he had grown up with. People who had been his scout and youth leaders when he was a kid. Most of his teachers from school. Church had always felt like coming home to him. Now Doug did not know what to feel. He loved his church, and had always accepted the doctrine without question. He still did love his church, but he was growing more and more concerned about the way his congregation would react if they ever learned the truth about Lucy.

Later on, in the men's meeting, the teacher, Brother Lewis, was discussing homosexual people. He said, "They are an abomination to God. Gays are evil, there is no doubt about it. Genesis 19 says that God condemns all homosexual behavior."

Doug thought about Lucy's mechanics. Nice women, trying to make a living and have a decent life. Could they really be evil, he wondered.

"Brother Lewis, I have a question," Doug cut in, "A lot of gays say that they were born that way. In this church, we are taught that God does not make mistakes. So I guess my question is, if God does not make mistakes, and people are born gay, how can we say that they are wrong?"

Brother Lewis looked stunned. The room was so silent that you could hear a pin drop, and Doug could feel many sets of eyes on him. "Well, I guess it depends on whether or not you can believe what the gays say about 'being born that way'. Personally, I don't." The teacher's voice was hard and mean. "Are alcoholics born that way? No. Are murderers born that way? No. It is all about resisting the influence of the Devil, and whether or not people are willing and strong enough to do it."

"So you are comparing gays to murderers?" Doug knew he should just let it go, but this guy was really getting under his skin.

"I am not comparing anyone to anything. I am just saying that if people are unwilling to follow the precepts of the bible, they will end up in hell where they belong." Brother Lewis stood in front of the room with his arms folded across his chest, like he was daring anyone to challenge him.

"You know, I don't really think that you have the right to make that call, Brother Lewis." This time it was Doug's turn to stare. A young man in the back of the room that Doug did not know very well had spoken.

"I am not making that call, the Lord is. Jude 1:7 says that all homo-sexuals will go to hell! Maybe you should learn your scripture before you start jumping all over on me." Brother Lewis was growing more and more defensive.

By this time, other members of the room were turning to argue with each other and look up scripture in their bibles. The room was getting louder and louder. What have I done, wondered Doug. He felt like this situation was his fault, yet he was not comfortable with sitting quietly, listening to hateful things being spread as doctrine. Finally, Doug spoke loudly. "Look, I wasn't trying to start a riot. I was just trying to point out that we all know gay people. We work with them, and some of us may have them in our families. All of us were created by God, and for that reason, I feel that we should all be treated equally."

Several other people agreed with him, and the class was dismissed.

స్త్ర

Doug decided to skip Sunday dinner at his parents house, and go straight to Lucy's. By the time he arrived, all of her guests from the night before had left. She was sitting on the porch swing typing on her laptop when he pulled up.

"Doug!" She closed her laptop and hurried down the stairs, throwing her arms around his neck. "I thought you would be going over to your par-ents house!"

"Well," Doug admitted, blushing. "I have been missing you a little, so I decided to come straight here."

"Well, I am so glad that you did! Are you guys hungry?" Lucy asked Emily and Brian. They both nodded. "Great, I was thinking about making a big pasta salad for lunch, plus I have some yummy cake leftover from last night. Does that sound good?"

Both kids agreed happily, then ran around the side of the house to find Luke and Hope, who were playing in the backyard. Doug followed Lucy into the house.

"Hey, I haven't see this Goddess before, have I?" Doug paused in front of a figure that looked like it had been made from clay and fired. She was about 12 inches tall, had a long swirling purple robe on, and long, dark hair. She had a long staff in her right hand, and a yellow orb in the other, uplifted hand.

"Oh, that is the Goddess Brigit. My friend Amy, who was here for Summer Solstice made her for me. Isn't she beautiful?"

"Yes, your friend Amy is really talented. Isn't there a Saint Brigit, as well?"

"Yes, they are one and the same. When the Christian church developed a stronghold in Ireland, while trying to convert the Druids, they adopted the Goddess Brigit as Saint Brigit to keep the peace."

"Really? I had no idea things like that were done." Doug was constantly amazed by Lucy's knowledge.

"Oh, yeah. A lot of stuff like that happened. Nearly all Christian holidays were Pagan holidays that received a makeover. Christmas, for example, was the Winter Solstice for thousands of years before it was Christmas."

"Wow. That is all news to me. How did it all happen?"

"Well, in the fourth century AD, the Roman emperor Constantine was seeking to bring internal peace to his empire. There was a lot of discord at that time between the old, pagan religion, and the new, Christian religion. Constantine knew that if he could blend the two religions together, he would be able to achieve a better level of peace and cohesiveness. He made Catholicism the official religion, but incorporated a lot of Pagan holidays and rituals in order to convince the Pagans to come around. He eventually forced all Pagans in his empire to be baptized into the Catholic church."

"Amazing. So, really, maybe Christianity and Paganism are not so different," Doug mused.

"I suppose in some ways that is true," Lucy agreed.

The rest of the day was spent playing ball with the kids, eating ice cream under the trees, and talking on the porch swing. Doug was getting so used to being at Lucy's house, he could not imagine things any other way.

"Oh, I keep forgetting to tell you that I am going out of town for a week," Lucy informed Doug, curled up with her head on his chest on the porch swing.

"You are? Where are you going?" Doug hated to hear that she would be gone for so long.

"Oh, just a quick book tour. I am going to do a couple of TV spots, a few speaking engagements, and stop at several New Age bookstores to sign books along the way."

"Are you taking the kids with you?"

"No, they are staying with Tina. It is too hard to travel with them." Lucy was starting to realize just how much she was going to miss Doug while she was gone.

"It is going to be weird without you around. Do you need any help with your yard or anything while you are gone?"

"Nope, I have a couple of friends who are going to stay here and house sit for me. That way, the chickens are watched over. They are treating it like a mini vacation."

"So, when are you taking off on your big adventure?" Doug had a knot in his stomach. A week without Lucy? This was going to be miserable, he knew.

"I fly out on Wednesday morning. I am planning on driving in to Denver on Tuesday though, to get the kids settled with Tina. I will stay over there Tuesday night."

ॐॐ

Monday night Doug and the kids met Lucy and her kids at a local restaurant for dinner. After dessert, Doug pulled a small wrapped package out of his pocket. "I have a going away gift for you," he said, handing the package to Lucy.

"Oh, Doug, how sweet of you!" Lucy tore the paper off to reveal a black velvet box. She eagerly opened the box. When she saw the contents, her eyes lit up. "Oh, Doug, this is beautiful!" She carefully removed a delicate, heart shaped ruby pendant on a thin, silver chain.

"I chose ruby because a wise author I know wrote that rubies help give people the courage to 'Follow their bliss', and I know that writing is yours. I hope that you have a wonderful time on your tour."

Lucy looked at him inquisitively. "Doug, have you been reading my books?"

"Well, yes, actually. I bought all of your books a few weeks ago. I am working on your 'Crystal Magic' book currently. I have learned a lot," he admitted.

Lucy blushed. "I can't believe you are reading my books. I am not sure whether to be flattered or embarrassed!"

"Oh, be flattered, for sure!" Doug stood up and clasped the chain around her neck, leaning over to kiss her cheek. He did not notice the group of people watching this exchange with interest a few booths over, nor did he hear them whispering about him. The truth was, the whole town had been taking notice of his relationship with Lucy.

chapter 8

Tuesday afternoon, Lucy and the kids loaded the car with their suitcases, and drove to Denver. Tina was waiting for them with open arms.

"Oh, you kids, we are going to have so much fun! I am planning on taking you to the zoo, the aquarium, on a hike, and a whole bunch more fun stuff!"

"Yay!" Hope hugged Tina tightly. "Can we go rock hunting, too? I promised Emily that I would bring her back a special crystal."

"Of course we can, sweetie." Tina was so happy to have these children as a part of her life.

Later, after the kids were tucked into bed, Tina and Lucy relaxed on the back porch with a glass of strawberry wine. Tina was always sure to have a bottle of strawberry chilled when Lucy came. It was her favorite.

"So, Lus, what's new?" Tina asked.

"Not much, just working on my new book during the day, and hanging out with Doug and his kids at night and on the weekends." Lucy was petting Tina's big Siamese cat, Oliver, who was stretched lazily out on her lap. Oliver had lived with Tina for as long as Lucy could remember.

"I had a really good visit with Doug at your house the other day. I really like him." Tina knew that her opinion mattered to Lucy.

"I do too. He is so good to me, and to my kids. His kids are very dear to me, as well." Lucy sighed. "I just worry."

"Worry about what, sweetie?"

"About where this is going. How can I stay undercover forever? I don't dare have anyone over to my house, I am very careful about what I say to anyone. I am not sure if I am just being paranoid, or if Rocky Point is going to freak out on me if they find out that I am a witch." Lucy took a sip of her wine.

"I wonder too," Tina agreed.

"You always taught me to be proud of who I am. I always have been, too. It was no secret in school that I was Wiccan. I have always been happy to be me.....and I still am. But now I am scared. I don't want to lose Doug because his town cannot accept me."

"Do you really think that will happen?" Tina's heart ached for Lucy, knowing that she could be facing major turbulence.

"I really don't know." Lucy stared out into the darkness.

"I have an idea, let's ask the cards," Tina said, walking into the house, and returning with a worn deck of Tarot cards. Tina loved this deck. She had been using it since her mother gave it to her when she turned thirteen.

She shuffled the deck three times, all the while asking the cards to show her what was happening with Lucy and Rocky Point. Then she fanned the cards out, and asked Lucy to pull out three cards, one past card, one present card, and one future card. Lucy ran her hand across the cards, pulling out the ones that felt right to her, and laying them face down in front of her on the patio table.

Tina turned over the first card, the past card. It was the Prince of Wands. "This is the ambition card. This card describes your move to Rocky Point. You were looking for somewhere to raise your kids that was quiet and rural, and you found it. It was a risk to move out of your comfort zone, but you accomplished it."

Then Tina turned over the second card, the present card. It was the Ten of Pentacles. "This card is the protection card. It is telling you to protect you and your family from harm. Lean on your friends and family, and draw support from past experiences."

Tina turned over the last card, the future card. It was the Tower card. "This card foretells of a coming crisis. The tower card always means that volatile energies will be unleashed. This card also tells us that after the storm, we will be liberated in some way."

Lucy let out her breath slowly. "So, basically, I needed to move to Rocky Point, currently I need to be protecting my family, and a rough time is coming."

"Yes, but you basically already knew that, didn't you?"

"I did, but I kept hoping that I was wrong. I just hope that my relationship with Doug will be able to handle it."

"It will, sweetie, it will," Tina reassured her, patting her hand.

Lucy tossed and turned all night. She had done enough Tarot readings to know that they were uncannily accurate. What was going to happen, she wondered.

෴

The next morning, Tina and the kids dropped Lucy off at the airport, bright and early. She was due in New York that afternoon to appear on "Book TV". They were doing a special segment on New Age authors, and she had been asked to participate. Lucy was honored to be asked to appear, and hoped that she would put in a good showing for her fellow Wiccans.

When she got off of the plane in New York, she took a cab to her hotel. After checking in and grabbing some lunch, she walked the five blocks to the studio that was expecting her. The sky scrapers, smog, and incessant flow of people made her feel closed in and uncomfortable. Lucy thought about the Ten of Pentacles and took a moment to protect herself from all of the energy swirling around her.

At the studio, she was ushered into a green room to wait for her turn to appear. The director, and older man named Bill, came in to speak with her. He explained that they would have a panel of five people ask her questions about her book, "Energy Work from a Wiccan Perspective" and she would have about twenty minutes to talk to them. The show would air on Sunday afternoon. Lucy was excited to get started, and really hoped that she would be able to represent the Wiccan religion well. To calm her nerves, she dabbed a couple of drops of sandalwood oil onto her wrists, then breathed it deeply into her lungs.

When Lucy was brought into the studio, she was placed at one side of a massive walnut table, with five people sitting across from her. There were two men and three women. She was shocked to realize that one of the men was a Catholic priest. She reached across the table and shook each of their hands and smiled at them.

The moderator, a middle aged man with short silver hair and glasses, sat beside Lucy. "Welcome, everyone, I am Phil Lerner, and this is Book TV. Our author today is Ms Lucy Meriweather, author of 'Energy Work From a Wiccan Perspective' and a practicing witch. Hello, Lucy, thank you for being here."

"Hello, Phil, it is my pleasure," Lucy responded, smiling, trying to fight the anxiety bubbling in her stomach. Why was there a priest here? As Phil went around the table and introduced the panel, Lucy's mind raced. She was not prepared to have a debate, and certainly did not want to have an ugly scene. The other members of the panel were an assortment of authors, English teachers, and a nurse. As she was thinking, she reached for her necklace. She was wearing the ruby from Doug. *"Rubies bring you the courage to follow your bliss,"* Doug had reminded her. She focused on the ruby and pulled as much strength from it as she could. She felt a surge of energy enter her through her heart chakra. Doug couldn't have known just how perfect this gift was.

"Lucy, before we begin, why don't you give us a summary of your book in your own words," Phil said.

"Energy work has been around for thousands of years, as has the Old Religion. This book describes the correlation between the two in the distant past, and in the present time. Just to clarify, energy work is basically the laying of hands on oneself, or another to pass energy into them, bringing about healing and well being."

"Great, well, let's go ahead and answer some questions from the panel, okay?" Phil was turning his attention to the men and women across the table.

"I have a question," the Priest began. "In your book you state that *'Ancient energy healing is the same laying on of hands blessing that many churches still practice today, often under the name of Priesthood.'*

"Yes, that is correct." Lucy knew where this was going.

"I find this statement to be inaccurate. The 'ancients', as you call them, were not worshiping the same God that modern churches worship. In fact most of them were worshiping the Goddess, isn't that true?" The priest was smiling, but his smile only thinly veiled his disdain for her.

"It is true that the ancients worshiped both the God and the Goddess, however, the God is, in fact, the same God that you worship. We believe that God and the Goddess have many names, but are still the same entity throughout time." Lucy could feel her confidence growing.

"Really? Well, I doubt that your God and mine are the same, but that is a discussion for another day. I also wonder why, in nearly all Christian churches, only men hold the Priesthood, and are capable of doing blessings and healings. In Wicca, women are permitted to do energy work as well as men. How can you, then, make such a comparison?"

He is making this too easy, Lucy thought. Women are way beyond being told that they cannot do the same things as men. "In Wicca, men and women are equal, as are High Priests and Priestesses seen as equals to the initiate. To take that one step further, we also believe that we are equal to plants and animals, not Lords over them. I should also add that women make tremendous healers. It makes sense that they would, considering that they are natural nurturers."

Finally, someone else cut in. A tiny, dark haired lady at the end. "Lucy, I want to say that I really enjoyed your book. I loved that fact that you made it very clear that all people can do energy work. In fact, I used the methods that you described on my garden last summer, and had the biggest bounty I have ever had. My question is this, doesn't the energy come from the universe, anyway? And if so, why does it matter what God or Goddess is worshiped by the healer?"

"Yes, you are correct that the energy is universal, but some believe that the universal energy that they are tapping into comes directly from their God. In truth, it doesn't really seem to matter where someone believes the energy is coming from, as long as they know how to call upon it."

"That makes sense," the dark haired woman agreed.

"We have to remember that Buddha, Jesus, and the Hindus all used energy work to heal. There are many who believe that ancient cultures such as Atlantis and Lemuria were much more proficient at energy work than we currently are." Now I am getting into the stuff I know, Lucy thought.

"So let me ask you then, how do you use energy work in your own life?" A man that Lucy believed was an English professor asked.

"I use energy work on my garden, yard and flowers. I use it on my children often, whether they are ill, or just having a hard day." Lucy smiled, "I send energy anywhere I see that needs a little extra love, like a sick neighbor, or a hurt dog."

As the panel continued to fire questions at her, Lucy responded confidently. By the end of the interview, she was feeling very good about the experience.

ॐ∽

Doug drove home from work Wednesday night feeling a little down. He had a meeting at church tonight, then figured he would just watch some TV with the kids. Lucy had only been gone one day, and he was already missing her. This was going to be a long week, he mused.

After a lengthy and boring budget meeting at church, Doug drove over to his parent's house to pick up his kids. "Hi honey," his mother, Cheryl, greeted him. "How was your meeting?"

"You know, same old, same old," he responded, kissing her on the cheek.

"Doug, the kids were telling me that Lucy is out of town. Is everything okay?" She sat down in her favorite arm chair in the living room.

"Oh, yes, things are fine," Doug sat across from his mother on the sofa. His dad, Bob, was already reclining in a chair in the corner, reading a book. "She will be back next week."

"Did she go on vacation?" Bob asked.

"Well, kind of. She is actually on a book tour." Doug shifted uncomfortably. "Lucy is an author."

"Really? I don't think that I knew that." Cheryl look surprised. "What has she written?"

"Oh, stuff about herbs and crystals, and things. She is really amazing at what she does." Doug was hoping that he could get by on that, without having to get into greater detail.

"Hmmm, well that is really nice dear. How are you handling her being away?" Cheryl could see that Doug was miserable.

"Well, okay, I guess. I am trying to deal with it, after all she just left yesterday."

"Doug, I have a crazy idea. Maybe you ought to surprise her, and show up to one of her book signings!" Cheryl had already watched her son go through the agony of losing his spouse. She was not interested in watching him writhe around missing Lucy as well.

"Oh, no. I couldn't do that. I have work, and the kids. I just couldn't." Doug was shocked that his mother would even suggest such a thing. She must be reading a bunch of romance novels again. "Besides, I don't want to look like some crazy stalker."

"Oh for goodness sake, son! Lucy is not going to think you are a stalker! Just go. What have you got to lose?"

"Seriously mom, I can't go!"

"Yes, you can go. I can keep the kids, and heaven only knows how much time off you have accumulated at work. Go, Doug. Be spontaneous!"

This, coming from the most conservative woman on the planet, Doug thought. "I don't know. What if she doesn't really want me there?"

"She does, I have no doubt of that. What do you think, Bob?"

Bob mulled the question over for a moment, then responded, "I think that Doug is a big boy, and that he can decide for himself what he should do."

"Thanks Dad," Doug said, happy to have some defense.

"I will say this, though," Bob continued. "Life is too short to be unhappy when you can do something about it. Doug, you obviously care about Lucy a great deal, and from the way she looks at you, she cares about you too. It would be good for you to take a chance now and then."

"Alright, tell you what," Doug told them, "I will think about it, and let you know tomorrow. Okay?"

"Okay, sweetie." Cheryl was glad that he was finally considering it.

On the way home, Doug was thinking hard about what to do. Sure, he would love to see Lucy. It would be wonderful to have some time to spend with her. I suppose that I could call Tina and find out what her itinerary is like, he realized. His thoughts were interrupted by the vibrating of his cell phone in his pocket. He was thrilled to see that it was Lucy calling. She told him all about Book TV, how scared she had been, how it all turned out well, and how she would be signing books in New York for two days, then on Saturday morning she would be flying to Boston for two days of book signings there.

"Did I really only leave yesterday?" Lucy asked.

"Yeah, but it seems like longer, doesn't it?" Doug replied.

"Oh, I have some friends who just got here to take me to dinner. I will call you tomorrow, okay?" Lucy said.

"Oh, sure, you have fun, okay?" Doug was not ready to hang up.

"Sure, I will...and Doug?"

"Yeah Lus?""

"I love you!" Lucy wondered if Doug could hear here heart pounding through the phone. She had never said that to a man before. Ever.

102

"I love you, too." He meant it too. Doug snapped his phone shut and walked out the patio to look at the stars. He loved Lucy more every day. Making a decision, he pulled his phone out of his pocket and dialed.

"Mark? Hi, it's Doug Brown. How are you? Good, good......hey, sorry for calling you after hours, but I have a quick question. Something has come up, and I need to take some vacation days from work, probably all of next week, in fact. Do you think that would work out?.....Okay, that sounds great. I really appreciate it.....No, everyone is just fine.....Does this have to do with Lucy? No, why do you ask?......Oh, you know Lucy is out of town?.......Well, I can't really talk about it right now, but I really appreciate the time off. See you tomorrow, goodbye."

Doug opened his phone and dialed again.

"Hi, mom. It's me, Doug. Oh, of course you know it is me....anyway, I was calling to say that I have decided to fly to Boston on Saturday to see Lucy. I am not sure how long I will be gone. A few days at least, maybe more. Does your offer still stand to take care of the kids?.......Okay, that sounds great. I will let you know when I get a plane ticket purchased.....Alright, calm down. I am glad too, thanks for suggesting it. Talk to you soon, bye."

Next, he rummaged around in the house for a list of emergency phone numbers that Lucy had left him. When he found it, he dialed his phone again, "Hi Tina, this is Doug Brown........Oh, yes, everyone is fine. How are the kids doing?.....Good, good, Brian and Emily are missing them already! The reason I am calling is that I have decided to fly to Boston on Saturday to surprise Lucy.....Do you think so? I am glad to hear you say that. I was hoping that she does not think I am trying to smother her........I was wondering if you know where she will be signing books on Saturday afternoon....Sure, I can hold." Doug was happy that Tina also thought his visit would be a good idea.

"Okay, Doug, it looks like she will be at a bookstore called 'The Bat's Wing' all afternoon. Here is the address," Tina was so excited to hear that Doug was going to see Lucy. She had left in a blue cloud, worrying about what the Tarot cards had said. A visit from Doug should cheer her up. "I also have the name of the hotel that Lucy will be staying in. Would you like it?"

On Thursday, Doug bought a one way plane ticket to Boston out of Denver, and booked a room for two nights in the same hotel as Lucy. He packed the kids' suitcases after work, then packed one for himself, being sure to pack plenty of clothes, since he had not decided how long he would be staying. If things went well, he was hoping to finish the tour with Lucy. After work on Friday, Doug took the kids over to his parents house, since he would be leaving early in the morning.

"Honey, are you sure you won't let your father drive you to the airport?" His mother had been fussing over him all evening.

"No, mom. Really. I will be fine. I would rather leave my car at the airport, so that no one has to come and get me."

After many hugs and kisses, Doug headed home to get some sleep. Just as he was dozing off, his phone buzzed. "Hi, Lucy!"

"Hi Doug, whatcha doin?" Lucy sounded tired.

"Just going to bed, actually. What are you doing?"

"I am going to bed now too, but it is two hours later here. Why are you in bed so early? Are you sick?"

"No, no, just tired, I guess. I need to get up early tomorrow to, uh, mow the lawn." Doug smiled. He could not wait to see her face tomorrow when he surprised her.

"Oh, okay, well I will call you tomorrow, then. Sweet dreams." Lucy was so tired. She had been signing books until her hand hurt, and her plane left early in the morning to fly to Boston. She was excited for Boston, though. She had several friends there, and they were planning on spending the weekend with her after her signings were done.

☙❧

When Doug's plane touched down in Boston, his stomach was filled with butterflies. He was hoping this was the right decision, and that Lucy would be happy to see him. He found a hotel close to the bookstore, checked in, and ate lunch in the hotel restaurant. After that, he decided to buy some flowers to take to the bookstore with him. He walked several blocks until he found a florist. By the time he got to the bookstore, there was a line out the door and half a block down the sidewalk.

"I wonder what all of these people are doing here," he thought as he headed in the door.

"Hey, buddy, what do you think you are doing?" A tall man with dreadlocks stepped in front of him.

"Oh, I am just coming to the book signing." Doug was a little bit intimidated by the man.

"So is everyone else here. The back of the line is down there," the man pointed.

"Oh, sorry, I had no idea that is what the line was for." Doug turned and hurried to the back of the line. He was dismayed to see how many men were also holding bouquets of flowers. After he took his place in line, he started listening to some of the conversations around him.

"I am so excited to actually get to meet her!" A teenage girl in front of Doug squealed. "Her books are absolutely amazing."

"I know," said a girl with her, who looked like she was in her early twenties. "I can't wait for her new one. Someone said it will be out in the spring. We are lucky to have her here. She doesn't tour very often."

"Yeah, from what I hear, she won't tour much because she has kids," said an old man behind Doug. "She doesn't really like to leave them."

Wow, thought Doug, Lucy has a bigger following that I realized. There were already at least ten people in line behind him. Some of the people in line looked really odd, purple hair, Mohawks, all black clothing, that sort of thing. Most of the people, however, looked completely normal. Doug fit right in to the crowd. After being in line for over an hour, he decided to talk to the people in line around him.

"So," he asked the girls in line in front of him. "What is your favorite book by Lucy?"

"Hmmm, that is tough, I love them all so much, but I think that I am going to have to go with, 'Why we are Wiccan,'" the older girl replied. "I have always felt a pull towards Earth Religions, from the time I was little. Lucy's book helped me to figure out why I felt that way, and how to proceed. It truly changed my life."

"That is amazing," Doug replied. "So, how did you proceed?"

"As soon as I turned eighteen, I joined a coven."

"So how did your family react to that, if you don't mind me asking." Doug was really intrigued by this story.

"At first they freaked out. My mom called the pastor over to do an exorcism on me, my dad quit talking to me. The whole town seemed to be against me for a while." She pushed her long red hair out of her face. "It was really hard, but my coven was there for me, and I knew that things would get better if I would ride it out."

"And has it?" Doug asked.

"Yes, it really has. My mom has gone from being afraid of Wiccan teachings, to being interested in them. My dad and I get along well on every level but this one, so we just don't talk about it much. As for the rest of the town, it blew over once it wasn't big news anymore."

"So, are you happy with your choices, then?" Doug asked.

She looked at him for a moment with her head tilted to one side, green eyes sparkling. "Yes, I am. I feel more at home, more like myself than I ever have. I realize that the way of the Witch is not for everyone, but it is the only path I can imagine myself on."

By then, the line had finally gotten to the door. Doug could see Lucy sitting at a table, greeting people, signing their books, giving an occasional hug. The line was still moving slow, but Doug was glad. It gave him a chance to watch Lucy work. She was so beautiful, so real. Doug kept his face hidden by the flowers as much as he could, not wanting Lucy to see him too soon. He took one of her books off of a rack near the table. He opened it up to the inside front cover, and waited for his turn. The exchange between Lucy and the red haired girl in front of him was so sweet. Lucy was very kind to her, and gave her a long hug.

When Doug walked up to the table, he handed her the flowers in a way that it blocked his face from hers. He slid the book into her hands in the same motion. Lucy lowered her head to write in the book. "Thank you for the flowers. Who do you want your book written to?"

"Uh, make it out to my love, who I have been missing." Doug waited in anticipation for her response.

Lucy froze, pen in hand. It couldn't be Doug. She look up curiously, then let out a giddy shriek. "Doug! Oh, I can't believe it!" By this time she was on his side of the table, pressing her lips to his. "What are you doing here?"

"Honestly, I just couldn't stay away. I know you have only been gone for a few days, but I have missed you so much. I flew in to Boston this morning."

"But how did you find me?" Lucy realized that there was still a long line of people waiting to see her, and returned to her side of the table.

"Tina told me where you would be this afternoon, and the rest is history. You have a lot of adoring fans waiting to meet you. Why don't you call me on my cell phone when you are done, and I will come back here and meet you?"

"Deal," Lucy said, standing to kiss him one more time.

Doug paid for his book, and started to leave. He was stopped by several people who had questions. "Are you married to Lucy?" "Are you Lucy's boyfriend?" and a common one, "Are you a high Priest in Lucy's coven?" He answered politely, and hurried back to his hotel. An hour later, his phone buzzed. Lucy was done, and ready to get together.

Doug walked back to the bookstore, and met Lucy inside as she was thanking the owners, and gathering up her things. "Wow, big crowd today, huh?" Doug commented as they walked out to the sidewalk.

"Not really. Sometimes stores have to end the signings because it is time to close and there is still a long line. Today, I made it all the way through." Lucy looked exhausted.

"Really?" Doug asked, astonished. He had no idea that Lucy was this popular.

"Yeah, I suspect that the signing tomorrow will be bigger, as it is at a much bigger store." Doug took Lucy's bag from her, noticing that she looked very tired.

"I hope you don't mind, Doug, but I had dinner plans with friends tonight. I would love for you to join us."

"Why would I mind, I dropped in on you." Doug knew that Lucy was excited to see her friends. "Are you sure that you want me to come? I could just catch up with you tomorrow for breakfast?"

"What? No way! You flew all this way to see me. Besides, we are not in Rocky Point. We can actually act like a couple in public here!" Lucy led him to her rental car. She drove them across town to a small restaurant called "The Ivy". When they got there, Lucy's friends were already waiting for them. There were three of them, a short, red haired man in his thirties, a taller blond Doug guessed to be in her late twenties, and an older, gray haired woman, probably in her mid fifties, Doug surmised.

After she had hugged each of them, she said, "Sean, Lettie, Maggie, I would like you to meet my boyfriend, Doug." Lucy smiled to herself, thinking how weird it was to say that. "Doug, these are my friends. I grew up with Sean and Lettie."

Doug shook each of their hands, smiling. After they were seated, Sean asked, "How was the book signing today?"

"It was good," Lucy replied. "I got to meet a lot of nice people, a few dissenters, the usual."

"Dissenters? Really?" Doug was surprised. "I did not realize there was any of that going on."

"Oh, sure," Maggie said. "There usually is at that sort of thing. Remember that time that lady threw garlic at you, Lucy? She thought she was going to drive the 'demon' out."

Everyone laughed except for Doug. "That is terrible. Who gave you trouble today?"

"Oh, it is no big deal, just some zealots trying to 'save me'. They were pretty tame as far as protesters go." Lucy dismissed it like it was nothing, but it bothered Doug.

"So, Lucy, I did not know you were dating," Sean said, with a mock pout on his face. "You always turn me down."

"Are you in Lucy's coven, Doug?" Asked Lettie.

"Me?" Doug blurted out. "No, of course not....I mean, no, that is not how we met."

Lucy laughed, "Doug and I met in the new little town I have moved to, Rocky Point. Our sons were on the same baseball team, we started hanging out with the kids, and...." Lucy shrugged, "and I fell hard for him."

"I see," said Maggie, patting Lucy's hand. "That is so nice. You have been alone for way too long."

"Thanks, Mags." Lucy had known Maggie since she was just a kid. She and her kids, Sean and Lettie, used to live in Denver, and belonged to her coven before they moved to Boston to be closer to Maggie's parents. It was always good to see them when she was in town.

The rest of the evening was filled with food, laughter, and catching up. Doug did not say very much, but really enjoyed listening to their stories about growing up Wiccan.

"It sounds like you all had a lot of fun," Doug commented.

"We did. It was a great way to be raised," Lettie smiled at Lucy. "You are the closest thing to a sister that I have ever had."

"Aw, I feel the same about you Let." Lucy yawned.

"You look really tired Lucy," Maggie remarked.

"I really am," Lucy responded, yawning again.

"Well, then, it is time to say goodnight," Maggie stood and hugged Lucy tight. "It has been wonderful to see you."

After all of the goodbyes had commenced, Doug and Lucy climbed back into the rental car. They drove in a comfortable silence to the hotel. Doug helped Lucy to her room, kissed her goodnight, and headed back to his room.

The next morning, Doug knocked on Lucy's door at 9:00 to take her to breakfast. They lingered over strawberry waffles, talking.

"Did I tell you about the Book TV interview?" Lucy asked.

"You mentioned it, but I would love to hear the details again," Doug replied.

"It went really well. When I got there I was so nervous, because there was a Priest in the panel of people that were there to interview me!"

"You're kidding? What did he say?"

"Not that much, actually. The other panel members were more supportive of me, and they monopolized a lot of the time. He asked me a couple of questions about energy work, for example, why it is that in Wicca, women are allowed to do it."

"What? Why would he say that?" Doug was surprised by this question.

"Well, because in Catholicism, men only are allowed to do 'Laying on of hands'."

"Oh, well, when you put it that way, I understand what he meant. That is the way it is in my church too." I wonder why that is, Doug pondered silently.

"It is that way in most churches, actually. How many other religions can you think of that have a High Priestess, for that matter." Lucy took a sip of coffee. "The thing is, women make excellent energy workers, because it is in their nature to want to nurture and heal others. Also, because women possess a deep, ancient power, that, when tapped, is phenomenal."

"I can see why women are excellent healers," Doug replied. "Do women posses any greater power than men?"

Lucy look surprised. "Well, I don't know if it is greater, but it is different."

"Okay, I can accept that." It was always interesting to hear Lucy's point of view.

"Speaking of religion, aren't you missing church today?" Lucy asked.

"Yes, I am." Doug was surprised that she said that.

"I'm sorry that you missed," Lucy said. "I know that you always go. Did you have a responsibility today?"

"Well, yes, I was supposed to help with a youth group, but I called the pastor and let him know that I would be out of town."

"That is too bad, you like working with the youth, don't you?"

"Well, yeah, but I want to spend some time with you. Are you sorry that I came?" Doug asked, confused.

"Oh, no! Of course not. I am thrilled that you are here. I just know that you worship on Sundays." Lucy reached over and grabbed Doug's hand. "I just want you to realize that just because I don't have a Sunday service is no reason for you to miss yours."

"Okay," Doug laughed. "I will be there next week, I promise!"

"Deal," Lucy leaned across the table to kiss him. She did not want to be the reason that Doug did not go to church. That could only make things more difficult for her.

"So, what is on the agenda today?" Doug asked, as they walked out of the hotel cafe.

"I have book signing at 1:00 at this great metaphysical bookstore and coffee shop called 'The Four Directions.' The owners are personal friends of mine. If you don't mind, I could really use a little help at this one. It will be much bigger than the one yesterday."

"Absolutely, what do you need?" Doug was happy to do anything for Lucy.

"Just stay with me, help with crowd control, get me a drink when I need one, that sort of thing. Yesterday I had no one sitting with me, so I was not able to get up and go to the bathroom the whole time!"

"Oh, that is not good!" Doug exclaimed. "I will stay with you."

"Shall we do some shopping while we wait?" Lucy suggested. "There is a lot of great shopping in Boston."

"Sure," Doug replied. "I promised my kids that I would bring them back a present. Maybe I will find something for them here."

chapter 9

APRIL JONES RELAXED in her favorite chair. She loved lazy Sunday afternoons. Since her husband was the Pastor in Rocky Point, he was usually still at church, in meetings for the afternoon. Her son was eating Sunday dinner at a friends house, so she had the whole house to herself. She clicked on the TV, and started browsing through the channels. Suddenly, she noticed someone she thought she recognized. She turned up the volume, curious. The host was speaking. No, she thought. It couldn't be. Still, she looks just like...

"...Ms Lucy Meriweather, author of 'Energy Work From a Wiccan Perspective' and a practicing witch. Hello, Lucy, thank you for being here."

Lucy Meriweather? It was her neighbor, Lucy. But a witch? April picked up the phone next to her chair and dialed. "Hi, Barb? Turn your TV on, you are not going to believe this. Channel 289...Yes, it is who you think it is!" April called Barb, Nelda, and Louise, who each called several people, who also called several people, and so on and so forth, until the nearly all of Rocky Point had their TV tuned in to channel 289.

"Okay, everyone, I hope that you are hungry," Cheryl sang as she carried a large pan of lasagna to the table where her whole family was waiting. Her whole family except for Doug. Just then, the phone rang.

"Hello," Bob answered. "What?.....No, I don't have the TV on. We are just sitting down to eat.....Why channel 289?......Lucy is what? You are talking too fast, Nancy. I can't understand you........Alright, I will turn it on. Okay, goodbye."

Bob hung up the phone and walked into the family room. "What is it, dear?" Cheryl asked.

"Nancy Withers just called to say that Lucy is on TV right now, channel 289." Bob turned the TV on to channel 289, and turned up the volume. Lucy, was in fact, on the show. The rest of the family was filling up the family room, trying to get a look at the screen.

"This is Book TV," Cheryl said. "I watch it in the evenings sometimes."

There was a blue box below Lucy on the bottom of the screen that read *"Lucy Meriweather, Author of Energy Work from a Wiccan Perspective."*

"A Wiccan perspective?" Repeated Liz. "What does that mean?"

"I think," said Brandon, "that means that Lucy is a Wiccan, or witch."

"No," said Cheryl. "How could that be? Lucy is so sweet!"

"I love Lucy," chimed in Emily. All of the adults turned to Emily, realizing that all of the children were in the room.

"Let's get all of you kids up to the table to eat," said Cheryl, ushering all of the children back into the dining room, then returning to the TV.

Everyone watched in disbelief as Lucy debated calmly with a priest, throwing light onto some of the starkest differences between them. The phone continued to ring with friends and church members calling. When the program broke for a commercial, Brian spoke first. "So this is where Doug is? Traveling around with some psycho, spreading her filth? What is the matter with him?"

"Maybe he doesn't know?" Suggested Liz hopefully.

"Yeah right!" David snorted. "Of course he knows. How could he not!"

"Remember that day that he said that he wanted to date Lucy, but couldn't because they had differing religions?" Nicole said. "Now we know what he meant."

"Oh, I feel so bad," Liz wailed. "I pushed him to date her. I had no idea that she was some devil worshiper."

"Was Doug really that lonely?" Asked Nicole. "I just can't get my head around this."

"How could Doug do this?" Brandon asked, angrily. "He has been spending all of his time over there. What about his kids, putting them in danger like this? I am disgusted with him!"

Cheryl and Bob were sitting quietly on the couch, Cheryl looked shocked. "I pushed him to take this trip, offered to take the kids. He has been so happy lately, and it was so nice to see him smiling." She shook her head, "And Lucy has been so sweet to me. She even helped me weed the garden one day."

Bob looked like he was contemplating this new information, but said nothing. Bob was the kind of guy who did not have much to say, but when he did speak, it was worth listening. He always gave good advice and was wise.

The phone rang again. It was April Jones, the pastor's wife. She said that the pastor had just received the news, and was terribly worried about Doug. He wanted them to come down to the church to speak to him right away. She had already called a teenager from down the street to come over and stay with the kids. Cheryl assured her that they would be right there.

When the Brown family arrived at the church, the pastor was waiting for them in his office. "Thank you all for coming. I know that you all must be as concerned about this situation as I am."

After everyone was seated, the Pastor began. "Witchcraft is extremely dangerous, and is directly linked to Satan. The fact that we have had a witch in our community for the last several months and did not know is a big concern to me. My best guess is that she has been in hiding here, maybe from the police."

"Oh my! You don't really think so?" Cheryl said in disbelief.

"I do," the Pastor said solemnly. "It is worse than that, though. I also believe that she has put Doug under some kind of spell to fall in love with her. She may be planning on turning him and his kids into demons."

"Oh, this is so scary," Liz said. "What can we do?"

"Well, first of all, we have to break the spell on Doug. I suggest that we call the whole church together to pray for Doug's soul. Hopefully that will do it."

"Okay, we can do that," Brandon said. "What else?"

"We also need to think about the safety of your families. Has she given any of you anything?"

"Yes," Cheryl said, looking frightened. She opened her purse and pulled out a small amber bottle. "She gave me this to put on bug bites and stings."

The Pastor opened the bottle and smelled it. "This could be some kind of brew that she made to turn you to the devil. It must be disposed of. Have you used any of it?"

"Yes, I have used it on me, and on Bob." Cheryl's face was white. "What is going to happen to me?"

"Nothing, Sister Brown," the Pastor assured her. "I will bless you and Bob, and clear the demons away from you. The Lord will keep you safe."

"I just don't understand. She was so nice. I did not get any negative feeling from her," Nicole said, shaking her head.

"It is true that things can look good on the outside, but be rotten on the inside," the Pastor agreed.

"Lucy has been to our house. Eaten at our table. She has helped me weed my garden and plant flowers. I cannot believe that I was so blind!" Cheryl was crying now. "And my poor Doug. Hasn't he been through enough? Losing his wife devastated him, and now he has been cursed, too. How much unhappiness can one person take?"

"I will come over and bless your house, in case she has left any evil magic there, but your garden is another story. She may have imbued your plants with her evil, in hopes that you would eat the harvest and turn to Satan. The garden must be tilled under, and the ground sterilized." The Pastor looked excited.

Cheryl wept quietly. "My beautiful garden. My son. How has this happened?"

"All right, that is enough!" Everyone jumped a bit at Bob's booming voice. "We don't need ourselves or our house blessed. We are NOT tilling our garden under. This is getting way out of hand."

"But Brother Brown," the Pastor started to say, but was interrupted.

"No, I have listened long enough, now you can all listen to me. What I see here is a young woman who leads a very different life that we do. She is obviously very intelligent, being a published author. She and Doug found some common ground somewhere, and fell in love. I will not entertain any ridiculous idea that she has put a curse on any of us, including Doug."

"But Dad," David said, "What if she has? Also, do you really want your son and grandchildren spending all of this time with someone who worships the devil? Like it or not, Lucy is a witch. That fact has not changed."

"I am not saying that it has," Bob said. "What I am saying is, you people are getting really paranoid. I am not going to let this turn into some

Salem Witch Trial. I would like to do some research about Lucy's religion myself before I come to any conclusions. In the mean time, there is a big dinner on the table at my house, and I am going home to enjoy it."

Bob stood and headed for the door. On his way past the Pastor's desk, he reached out and grabbed the small amber bottle. "I will be keeping this. It works great on mosquito bites!" Reluctantly, the rest of the Brown family filed quietly out behind him.

"If you need anything at all, please call me," the Pastor said to Cheryl as they walked out. "I will be praying for all of you."

After the Browns had left his office, the Pastor picked up the phone. "Hello Brother Larsen, this is Pastor Jones. We have a big problem. I just met with the Browns.....It did not go well....I have reason to believe that Bob has already been turned. He would not let me bless him.....He also said that he would not let me bless their house...He even acted sympathetic to the witch....I agree, this could be very serious.....Will you please start a phone tree? We need to call every member of the congregation and let them know that we will be praying for the Brown's, especially Doug and Bob, to save their souls. Great, thanks a million, good bye."

Brother Larsen hung up the phone, and called the next person on the phone tree, who called the next person, and so forth. By the time the message from the Pastor had gotten around the phone tree, it sounded like this, "Hello, Sister Wood? I am calling with an urgent request from Pastor Jones. It seems that Doug and Bob Brown have both been turned into sorcerers by a witch who serves Satan. It is contagious, and so everyone is being admonished to wear necklaces made from garlic if they go out in public. Also, we have been asked to pray for our souls so that we do not get stricken by the devil."

≈∽

On the way home from the church, no one spoke much. Everyone was lost in their own thoughts. Cheryl was feeling very shaken. She kept playing the Pastor's words over in her head. Curses, brews, love spells. Could any of this be real? If it was real, what was going to happen?

Liz was thinking along the same lines. Was the Pastor right? Could it be that Doug was actually not operating under his own free will? I am not sure about any of this, Liz thought. Lucy is so sweet and kind, could she really be evil?

Brandon's jaw was clenched. What was Doug doing with this woman? Was he giving up his religion to be with her? I am afraid that this could tear our family apart, Brandon thought. And yet, his dad was not getting too worked up about it, and Brandon had always trusted Bob's judgment.

Bob was thinking hard, too. Doug was a smart kid, always had been. He would not get wrapped up into something that was dangerous. Surely he has already done his homework, Bob thought. Just as he turned onto his street, he had an idea. He slammed on the breaks, spun the wheel, and did a u-turn.

"Why are we here, Bob?" Cheryl asked as he swung the car into Doug's driveway.

"I need to see something. Everyone just stay in the car." Bob used the key under mat to let himself in. He walked straight to Doug's computer desk. There were four books sitting there that were written by Lucy Meriweather. Perfect, Bob thought. I knew that my son would have been doing some research. This is exactly what I needed. He put the books in Doug's briefcase to keep his family from seeing the titles, then returned to the car.

"What did you find, dad?" David asked him.

"Just some research that Doug has been doing. I would like to see things from his point of view."

"Tell you what, when you have it figured out, let me know," Brandon spat. "Until then, I don't want anything to do with that jerk."

"Me neither," David added. "I don't know what he is up to, but I am sure not going to let it rub off on my family!"

"Oh, boys," Cheryl cried. "Please don't be like that. Doug may need us more now than ever."

Doug held Lucy's hand from across the table as they waited for their lunch. They had chosen a small café near the Four Directions Bookstore to eat before the book signing. Lucy was looking out the window. "Doug, I am getting a bad feeling about something. There is something wrong at home."

"With your kids?" Doug asked.

"No, I don't think so. It feels like Rocky Point to me." She looked Doug in the eyes, looking troubled. "Can you call your mom and check on the kids?"

"Of course," Doug pulled his phone out of his pants pocket and dialed. The phone rang and rang, finally getting voice mail. "No one is home, I will call later," Doug assured Lucy.

Lucy nodded. She felt sick inside. This was the same feeling she had gotten when Luke had been injured at school, and when Tina had been mugged while in San Francisco a few years ago. She tried to eat her salad, but had lost interest. Finally, she sighed and looked at her watch. "We better get going to the book signing."

The book signing was just as big as Lucy predicted. Doug was, again, amazed at the long lines of people lined up, waiting to meet Lucy. When Lucy needed a break, he roped off the signing area. While she was away, he visited with a lot of interesting people.

Later that evening, Bob sat in his office, reading Lucy's books and taking notes. It was becoming more and more clear to him that Lucy was not a devil worshiper in any way. In fact, her religion seemed to be much more about nature and the earth than anything else. Lucy was a skilled writer, and her books were easy to read and understand. Bob wrote notes on a legal pad as he read, compiling a list of things that Lucy is, and a list of things that Lucy is not. So far, Lucy is: An excellent author, very educated about her subject matter, a Wiccan, a good mother, a goddess worshiper, a nature lover, a healer. The "Lucy is Not" column said: A devil worshiper, evil, and dangerous.

Just then, the phone rang. Bob sighed when he saw Doug's name on the caller ID. He answered quickly before Cheryl could get to the phone. "Hi son, how is it is going?" He tried his best to sound cheerful.

"It is going good dad, I just wanted to check on the kids. Is everything okay at home?"

"The kids are just fine Doug. They are having a blast." Bob was determined to tell Doug anything he had to in order to keep him on his trip. He certainly did not deserve to have his trip ruined by bad news.

"Okay, is everyone else alright?" Doug knew Lucy's feelings were usually accurate. His dad's voice seemed to be a little strained as well.

"Positive!" Bob insisted.

Doug assured Lucy that all was well at home, but she was not convinced. "I still feel off, like something serious has happened."

The next morning, Doug and Lucy boarded a plane bound for Arizona. Lucy was due to speak at an energy workers conference in Sedona, Arizona that evening. They flew into Phoenix, then rented a car and drove to Sedona.

"Doug, I am so excited to be in Sedona. This is a magical area for me." Lucy was looking at all of the red rock hills around her as they neared the little town.

"The red rocks are beautiful, for sure. What else is so great about Sedona?" Doug asked.

"There are energy vortexes all over the town, and they are really amazing to experience. I am hoping we have time to visit a few of them before we have to go."

"Energy vortexes?" As usual, Doug was learning something new.

"They are spots where the energy feels more intense than in other places. To me, some of them are very calming, while others are very energizing. There is one that always makes me cry, releasing old emotions and feelings."

"Really?" Doug said, "But how do you know they are there?"

"By meditating, slowing down your mind, and just allowing yourself to have the experience. Thousands of people every year come to Sedona to experience the vortexes for themselves. Many people report having life altering experiences here." Lucy was looking out the window with a dreamy look on her face. "I had forgotten how much I love it here."

After they checked into their hotel, Doug and Lucy grabbed some lunch, then drove to a vortex called Airport Mesa. Lucy said that it was an easy one to get to, and a great way to start. They parked the car and hiked to the very top of a tall red rock. Once at the top, Lucy sat down near the edge. Doug joined her, amazed by the view.

"Wow! You can see the entire valley from here."

"I know, it is beautiful, isn't it?" Lucy crossed her legs and placed her hands on her thighs, open palms up. "Do you want to feel the vortex, Doug?"

"I don't know if I can, but I am willing to try," Doug followed suit, crossing his legs and placing his hands in position, feeling a little silly.

"Close your eyes," Lucy instructed. "Good, now tip your head back a little bit. You need to get centered and grounded. I want you to take a deep breath in, then let it out slowly. We will do this ten times. Every time you breath in, I want you to picture yourself sinking deeper into the rock, becoming more and more at one with the earth." Lucy's voice was quiet, almost whispering.

Doug began breathing in and out slowing, trying to follow instructions. By the sixth breath, he was feeling a little light headed. By the eighth breath, he was feeling very heavy and relaxed. By the tenth breath, he felt like he was barely conscious. Lucy's voice seemed very far away when she told him to stay still and enjoy the moment. He was not sure how long he stayed in the meditation. It seemed like time was unimportant. He had never felt so safe, or so strange. Even though his eyes were closed, he felt like he was seeing colors swirling around him. Even though he knew that there were other people around him, climbing to the top of the vortex, talking, and taking pictures of the fantastic view, he was barely aware of them. He felt like he was wrapped up in a cocoon, a bubble.

Finally, he started to become more aware of his surroundings. He noticed that he was sitting on a sharp rock that was poking him. He shifted, and opened his eyes. Lucy was sitting next to him, watching him. Doug stretched and yawned. Lucy smiled at him, but said nothing. She leaned over and rested her head on his shoulder. Doug wrapped his arm around her. The two sat in silence, taking in the energy and enjoying the moment of peace. Finally, Doug spoke.

"That was the most amazing experience I have ever had. I think that I really did feel the energy from the vortex."

"You seemed to be in a good place," Lucy agreed. "How did it feel?"

"Well, it felt amazing. It is hard to put it all into words. I felt really safe, really connected to something outside of myself. For a while, I thought that I could stay there forever."

Lucy was astonished by Doug's ability to feel and sense energy. She was reminded of the time that he could feel the energy coming from the amethyst cathedral in her altar room. "I am so glad that you had a good experience. What happened is that you became very grounded, therefore a connection with the earth's energy was forged. Some people have a very difficult time learning to meditate, but you picked it right up."

After Lucy and Doug hiked back down to the car, they drove back to their hotel to clean up for Lucy's speaking engagement. They decided to walk to the venue, since it was so beautiful outside.

"So, tell me what this conference that you are speaking at is all about."

"Well, this conference is for energy workers. Reiki, specifically."

"What is Reiki?" Doug had seen Lucy do energy work before, but did not really understand it.

"Reiki is a technique of energy healing that is probably the best known. The founder of Reiki was named Mikau Usui. He lived in Japan. His system eventually made it to Hawaii, then to the upper forty eight states. Since then, many different people have designed other forms of Reiki as well." Lucy paused, "The thing is, universal energy is out there for everyone to benefit from. It just takes learning a system so that you can harness it."

"Really? So you are saying that anyone could do energy healing if they wanted to?" Doug was surprised. He thought that this kind of stuff was reserved for psychics only.

"Of course. We all have the same abilities. Some people pick energy work up easier than others, of course, but that doesn't mean that they cannot learn. Learning to do Reiki or some other form of energy work can really enrich people's lives."

By this time, Doug and Lucy had arrived at a large, adobe style hotel with a sign in the lobby that read, "Energy Healing Convention" with an arrow. When Lucy walked in the door she was greeted by a tall, older man.

"Lucy! I am so glad that you could make it!" He said, leading her to the registration table. Doug followed behind, again feeling like he was in a completely foreign place. "Here is your badge and an itinerary of events," the man was saying to Lucy.

After they walked away from the table, Lucy turned to Doug. "I still have an hour until I speak. Why don't we go walk around the Hands on Hall. There are a lot of great healers here with booths."

As they browsed around the hall, many people smiled at Lucy, some greeted her by name. There were a lot of different things going on. At one booth, there was a woman laying on a massage table with different stones laid out on her body. The sign said "Chakra Balancing with Crystals $25.00." There was a woman holding her hands above each crystal for a few moments before moving on to the next one. Doug was watching with interest.

"You ought to try it," Lucy urged. "It can be an intense experience."

"I am not sure what Chakras are," Doug admitted. "I remember reading something about them, but I am still not sure."

"The body has certain spots where energy exits and enters," Lucy explained. "They are called Chakras. The word chakra is Sanskrit for 'wheel'. Chakras operate like wheels, or disks, spinning. People have 7 main chakras, that run down the body, plus more chakras in the feet and palms."

"Why do they need to be balanced?" Doug asked, gesturing to the woman on the table.

"Each chakra is linked to a certain part of the physical and emotional body. When a persons chakras are not functioning properly, they are struggling in visible ways like poor physical or emotional health." Lucy loved that Doug was always asking questions. "For instance, if someone is struggling a lot with stomach issues, the healer would be concerned with the Solar Plexus, which is the right above the belly button. The Solar Plexus deals with emotions such as self esteem and self worth."

"Wow, that makes me think about a time when Brian was dealing with a bully at school. He was constantly having tummy aches. I thought that he was faking because he did not want to go to school. Now I am wondering if his self esteem was suffering, thus bringing on the tummy aches."

"That could definitely have been the case," Lucy agreed.

"Why are they using crystals to balance them?"

"Chakras have a vibrational quality that responds to the vibrational quality of crystals. We use crystals whose color matches that of the Chakra. The Chakra will adjust itself to match the crystal. The healer is sending energy through the crystal to help with the process. When all of the Chakras are done, she will send energy through them, starting at the root, to make sure that the energy is flowing well."

"How does she know?" Doug was still really unsure of all of this metaphysical stuff.

"Why don't you ask her?" Lucy suggested. "It looks like she has just finished up with her client."

Doug hesitated. It was one thing to learn about this stuff from Lucy, but to sit down with a complete stranger and ask questions made him nervous. He trusted Lucy, after all.

"Hi," the woman said, smiling. "I am Shannon. You look like you have some questions."

"Well, yeah, I guess I do." Doug shook Shannon's hand. Lucy, he noticed, had stepped over to another booth to speak with someone. "My girlfriend was explaining to me what Chakras are. I understand the idea of Chakras, but I still don't get how you know when they are out of whack."

"Okay, I can help you with that." Shannon motioned Doug to a chair and sat down across from him. "Have you ever had a traumatic experience, and then not felt like yourself for a long time?"

"Well, yeah." Doug shifted, feeling very uncomfortable.

"Can you tell me about it?"

"I guess so. It was when my wife died. It was all so sudden, everything happened so fast..." Doug lapsed into thought. He started thinking about the way he felt shaky and weak for months afterwards. His mother said that his head was in the clouds. He could barely function most of the time. But why was Shannon asking him about this, he wondered.

"Sure, a death is a something that can really throw your energy off kilter. That would have really messed up your heart and root chakras, especially. Your root chakra is where you keep your feelings of safety and security. How do you think that your wife's death affected your root chakra?"

I didn't know I was going to get a pop quiz, Doug thought. "I was scared of losing someone else, worried that tragedy would strike again. I had a hard time concentrating or getting anything done."

"Of course," Shannon nodded. "How long did those feelings last?"

"About six months, then I started feeling more like I could handle things." Doug thought for a minute. "So are you saying that my root chakra was affected by my wife's death to such a degree that I felt it physically?"

"That is exactly what I am saying." Shannon looked excited, glad that he had gotten her point.

"Okay, I can accept that. I can even see a correlation between those feelings and other times when I had a trauma and felt the same way.

The thing is, I have never had my Chakras balanced, yet eventually I end up feeling better. How can you explain that?"

"Your energy system has, over time, managed to balance itself. Most people do. Occasionally, though, people don't. Then their unbalanced system results in disease, both mentally and physically." Shannon took a deep breath. "How am I doing? Am I answering your questions so far?"

Doug cocked his head to the side, thinking. "Yes, but I still am wondering about one thing. When you work on a client, you use crystals to balance their energy, right?"

"Right, along with Reiki."

"Okay, so how do you know it is working?" Doug hoped he was not offending the healer by asking so many questions.

"I watch the process unfold. When I am done, I can tell the client what Chakras were out of balance, and sometimes I can tell them what kind of issues they are having that is causing the imbalance." Shannon smiled to herself. This guy was obviously genuine, and really looking for answers.

"You watch it how? I can't see anything happening at all."

"It is a mental picture. It is really a combination of feeling things, seeing things, and having an inner knowing of things." Shannon had explained her gift many times. Some people understand, and some just don't.

"Alright, I am willing to give it a try," Doug handed Shannon the money, and she directed him to the massage table.

Lucy walked out of the hall to prepare for her speech, smiling about Doug, still on the massage table with stones lined up on his body. She was wondering to herself how she had found someone as open and great as Doug. Soon, Lucy found herself standing on a stage with in front of a crowded auditorium of people. She took a deep breath, smiled, and began, "Good afternoon......"

৵৵৽

Doug looked at Lucy, sleeping in her airplane seat. He was, again, overwhelmed by his feelings for her. What an amazing person she was. This trip had been an enriching, exciting experience for Doug. He had been blown away by the sincere people he had met. And they all shared a common bond. They all loved Lucy. Doug's thoughts were interrupted by the flight attendant giving landing instructions. He gently roused Lucy, and they prepared to land in Denver.

When Doug pulled up to his parents house, his kids ran to the car to meet him. He kissed them both, then headed in to see his parents. "Oh Doug, thank goodness you are safe," his mother exclaimed, hugging him tightly in the living room.

"Of course I am safe," Doug replied, puzzled.

"Doug, you better sit down," Bob began. "There has been some commotion around here since you have been gone."

Doug sat down on the couch, wondering what could have happened to make his mother so anxious and his dad so serious. Bob cleared his throat. "Son, it has come to the attention of the whole town that Lucy is a....a witch."

The blood drained from Doug's face. "What? How?"

"So you knew?" Cheryl cried out. "You knew all along that Lucy is a witch and you dated her anyway? How could you, Doug?"

"How could I what?" Doug snapped, feeling defensive. "How could I fall in love with an amazing woman? It was really easy, if you want to know the truth."

"You have exposed your children to evil, your family to evil. I don't even know you any more." Cheryl sank into a chair, dabbing at her eyes. "What kind of father does this?"

"Mom! That is not fair. The kids love Lucy. You did too, until you found out she was different from you." Doug put his head in his hands. How had such a wonderful week turned into this mess?

"Okay, Cheryl, that is enough." Bob broke in. "Doug needs to hear the details, and we need to give him a chance to talk."

"Thanks dad," Doug said. "What happened?"

"Well, last Sunday the Pastors wife saw Lucy on Book TV. I am assuming that was a part of her book tour?"

Doug nodded, feeling numb.

"She called a few people, who called a few people, and so on. By the time the interview was over, the entire town was watching. The pastor called us in to his office. He seems to think that Lucy is worshiping the devil, and that she has put some sort of spell on you." Bob choked back a chortle.

Cheryl glared at Bob. "It is not funny, Bob."

"Actually, I think it is pretty funny. There has been total madness here all week. I went to the grocery store to buy a few things for dinner. They are sold out of garlic. Seems that someone decided that witches are also vampires."

"But being a witch has nothing to do with worshiping the devil," Doug protested. "When I first learned who Lucy is, I reacted like the rest of the town. I was scared, and a little weirded out. The thing is, I really liked Lucy. I could not get my head around the idea that Lucy could be evil in any way. I bought all of Lucy's books, plus did a lot of internet research. What I discovered is that Wicca is really all about loving the earth, your family, your community, and so forth. There is no devil in that religion, let alone the worship of one."

The room fell silent for a few moments, then Cheryl spoke. "Doug, your dad has told me all of that already. I am still having a hard time with it. After all, I have been taught all of my life that Pagan religions are evil, wrong somehow. It is hard to turn back the clock and change my beliefs."

"I know, mom. Believe me, this has not been an easy process for me either. My heart has been urging me forward, but my head has been holding me back. I even tried to stop seeing her, but I was miserable. So were the kids. All I want is to love someone who loves me back. I have that with Lucy. We make each other happy." Doug felt like he needed his mother to understand why he made the choices that brought them to this point.

"When my wife died, I was devastated. I could not imagine myself ever loving anyone else. I was sure that I would be alone for the rest of my life."

"I know, son. My heart broke for you every day. I could feel your pain, your suffering. I have hoped for years now that you would find happiness." Cheryl sighed. "This, however, is not what I had in mind at all."

A heavy, uncomfortable silence hung in the air. Doug had a million thoughts swirling around in his head. He knew that this would change everything. What did I expect? He wondered. Did I really think that we could keep on like this forever, flying under the radar?

"Mom, you are the most Christ like person I have ever met. You have always been kind, loving, and charitable. I have to believe that Jesus did not intend for people to persecute and hate each other in his name. Wouldn't you agree?"

"I am not sure it is right or fair for you to bring my faith into this," Cheryl said coldly. "But no, I am certain that was not the kind of thing that Jesus would have condoned."

"Why, then, is it okay for the town to turn on Lucy like this? She has been very good to you and dad. She has been a wonderful neighbor. If she were Christian, we would not be having this conversation."

Bob cleared his throat. "I hope that you don't mind, but I went to your house and borrowed your books by Lucy. I have read most of them, and taken a lot of notes. I have come to the conclusion that Wicca is neither evil or dangerous. My feelings for Lucy have not changed. She is welcome in our home and in our family." Cheryl tried to object, but Bob held up his hand. "No, Cheryl. I mean it. I will not be a part of this foolishness, and neither should you."

"Thank you Dad. I want to apologize to both of you. I did not mean for you both to be pulled into any drama with the town or the church. I have been wanting to talk to you about it, but just did not know how you two would react." Doug was relieved to have his dad behind him. He was hoping that his mother would come around also. "The real question now is, how do we handle the town and the church? Will they listen to reason?"

"I hope so." Bob responded. "The people in this town are good folks. They are just scared, and misinformed. Right now, they are feeling hurt, like they have been deceived. Lucy was their friend, someone they trusted. Now they feel like she has lied to them, maybe even tried to harm them."

"Harm them?" Doug was pacing back and forth in front of the couch now. "It is ludicrous to think that Lucy would ever harm anyone!"

"Of course it is, dear," Cheryl agreed. "I may be struggling with Lucy's beliefs, but I agree that she is not dangerous. That sounds so silly, doesn't it?"

"You need to be prepared though, Doug. A lot of people from the church have been praying for your soul and things like that. There are some really crazy rumors going around." Bob shook his head.

"Where are they getting their ideas from, anyway?" Doug was feeling protective of Lucy.

"Unfortunately, the pastor has been doing a lot of talking. He seems to be enjoying this. He has even offered to do special blessings on anyone who has had any contact with Lucy to 'drive the evil out'. He tried to do it to your mom and me, but I wouldn't hear of it."

"What do you think I should do?" Doug asked quietly, looking at his hands.

"I think that you should continue to live your life, son. This will blow over in time. Tell people the truth if you feel like it is their right to know it. Otherwise, keep you head down and go about your business. Hopefully, if you and Lucy keep a low profile for a little bit, this will all go away." At least I hope so, Bob thought to himself.

chapter 10

LUCY SETTLED INTO a chair on the patio with a cup of coffee. She was so happy to be back from her trip. Tina, Megan, and Amber were also sitting on the patio with cups of coffee.

"So, how was your trip?" Megan asked.

"It was great,'" Lucy replied. "I got to meet a lot of wonderful people."

"One wonderful person especially, right Lus?" Giggled Amber.

"What are you talking about?" Lucy turned her gaze on Tina.

"Oh, alright, so I told them about Doug surprising you. We are all just so excited to see you so happy!" Tina ducked, avoiding the pillow that Lucy had hurled at her.

"Okay, so Doug met me in Boston and finished the tour with me. So what?"

"So what?" Megan repeated. "Are you kidding me. The guy leaves his kids and his job to fly halfway across the country for you, and all you have to say is, so what?"

"You are not getting off that easy!" Amber declared. "We want details! Start dishing."

"Oh, alright, nosey." Lucy laughed. "I was signing books in Boston when someone hands me flowers and asks me to sign a book 'To my love, who I have missed.' I looked up in surprise because it sounded just like Doug, and to my total amazement, it was."

"Oooooh, wow! That is so sweet. I can't believe he did that!" Megan exclaimed. "That has to be one of the most romantic things that I have ever heard."

"Yeah, great. Romantic, sure." Amber agreed. "But the real question is, how was the sex?"

"What?" Lucy shrieked. "Amber, I can't believe you are asking me that."

"Why?" Amber laughed. "Lucy, you are in your 30's. It is okay for you to sleep with your boyfriend, you know."

"I am aware of that, Amber. But the truth is, there was no sex."

"Yeah right!" Megan shook her head. "Now you are lying to us. No man goes to the lengths that Doug did to come to see you and not have sex. No way, no how. Not happening."

"Doug's church does not believe in sex before marriage," Lucy explained. "Seriously."

"But yours does," Megan said seductively, grinning.

"Doug has been amazingly accepting of me and my beliefs. I owe him the same." Lucy said sternly. "Besides, there is a lot more to a relationship than sex, you know."

"Of course there is. You can still hold hands and pass notes in class, right?" Amber laughed. "Just kidding. I think that it is pretty great that you and Doug can find common ground and put your religious views aside."

"So do I," Tina agreed. "Something tells me that you and Doug will find a way to integrate your lifestyles into something that works for both of you."

"I really hope so," Lucy sighed. "Sometimes it feels like we are playing this forbidden game. It is fun and exciting, but it will come to an end. I just hope that Doug's family can come to accept me for who I am at some point. I really don't like all of these secrets and half truths."

"Stay positive, Lucy," Tina reminded her. "It is better to focus on what you want, rather than on what you don't want. Work on attracting acceptance and peace."

"Okay," Lucy smiled. "I will."

⊱⊰

A few hours later, Lucy and the kids were driving back to Rocky Point. Hope was keeping Lucy entertained with stories about all of their adventures with Tina when her cell phone chirped. It was a text from Doug, asking Lucy not to go home, but to come straight to his house instead. "How odd," Lucy thought. "We had both agreed to see each other tomorrow, since we both need to spend time with our kids tonight."

When Lucy walked into Doug's house, she could feel the tension. Doug was sitting at his desk, writing an email on his laptop. When he saw Lucy come in, he shut his computer and strode over to Lucy and held her tightly.

"Hi Luke, hi Hope," Doug smiled at the kids. "There are two kids in the backyard who are going to be really happy to see you guys!"

Luke and Hope headed outside to find their friends. Doug led Lucy over to the couch. She sat down, wondering what in the world would make Doug's energy feel like this.

"What is wrong Doug? Is your family okay?"

"Yeah, they are fine. There has been some trouble while we have been gone, though."

"What kind of trouble?"

"The pastor's wife saw you on Book TV. The whole town knows our secret."

"How has the reaction been?"

"It sounds pretty bad. My parents have had the pastor trying to exorcise them of evil, things like that."

"Really? Wow. So people actually think that I am dangerous or something?"

"Unfortunately, yes, some people do."

Lucy groaned, "I should have seen that coming. I should have never done that interview!"

"Why?" Doug asked. "This was bound to happen at some point. Besides, you were proud of that interview. You felt like you did great job representing Wicca. Why should you have to feel bad about that?"

"Because I have hurt your family. Because I have hurt you." Lucy tried to swallow the massive lump in her throat. "I am so sorry Doug."

"No! I don't want you to apologize!" Doug took Lucy by the shoulders and looked into her eyes, "You have changed my life. I have found myself after being lost for the last three years. Please don't apologize for that."

Lucy laid her head on Doug's chest. "What do you think is going to happen?"

"I am not really sure. My dad thinks that we should just live our lives, and keep a low profile. Maybe this will all go away if we give it a little bit of time."

Lucy was quiet for a long time. Finally, she spoke. "Doug, I have been trusting my intuition ever since I met you. It has not failed me yet. I keep getting the craziest impression of what we should do."

"Really? What? I am willing to try anything!"

"Well, I have faith in the universe. I believe that if I cast a certain spell, or send out energy for a certain purpose, then I will get that which I am seeking."

"Okay, I respect that," Doug said. "What are you thinking?"

"You have faith in Christ, right?"

"Yes, I do."

"Then I think that we should both deal with this according to our faith." Lucy's eyes shone with excitement. "It has to work. I will do spell work, and you will pray!"

Doug eyes widened, and he laughed. "You're right. This is crazy!"

"I know how it sounds," Lucy agreed. "But I think that we should try."

"What do you think I should pray for?"

"Well, I was going to leave that up to you. I am not really sure how one addresses Jesus."

"Oh, sure. Okay. What are you going to do?"

"I am going to bless this town. We can't fight hate with more hate. It will just cause more bad energy. I will shower the town in love and light.

It might take some time, but I am feeling very sure that with our combined efforts, we can do a lot of good. The very best thing will work out for us." Lucy stood, "In fact, I am going to head home right now to get started. Our love is a good thing. We can use it to create peace Doug. I am sure of it!"

Doug kissed Lucy and the kids good bye, put his kids to bed, then headed to his room to pray. Lucy did not know how much she was asking of him. Doug had not prayed since his wife died. He had been so mad at God for so long. He had been going through the motions at church but wasn't really doing his part. Lucy did not know that, though. Nobody knew that. She just knew that their faith in their own deities and in each other would see them through this. Doug knelt next to his bed a took a deep breath.

"God, it's me, Doug Brown....uh, I guess you probably already knew that though, huh? Well, uh, it has been a while, hasn't it? I don't really know what to say. I just need to ask you to help me. You sent an angel into my life God. She has healed my wounds and given me back the life I thought that I had lost for good. The trouble is...oh, what am I saying? You know what the trouble is. I don't know what to do. I can't lose Lucy over this. I can't stand the thought of it. I don't know how to reconcile my family and my church with Lucy and her beliefs. She is the one who told me to pray. Seems kind of funny now that I think of it. Well, anyway, if you can help me here, I would sure appreciate it. Lucy says that we need to ask for love for everybody. I am having a hard time feeling love for people who are turning on Lucy and me, but I will try. And I will drop in more often. I know that my absence has not been good for me. So, thanks, and, uh, Amen. I mean, in Jesus name, Amen."

Lucy had a lot to think about on her way home. She knew that this day was coming, but she had not known how she would handle it. "I think that I will call on all of my Reiki friends to send love to Rocky Point. That is a good way to start. I will figure out a spell that I can carry out tomorrow."

When she was two blocks from her house, Lucy could see the flash of red and blue lights in her rear view mirror. She checked her speedometer, but she was not speeding. "Odd, I wonder why I am getting stopped," she wondered, as she pulled off to the side of the road.

The officer approached her car and shined a bright light in her eyes. "License and registration please." Lucy produced the documents. The officer took them without speaking and walked back to his car.

"Mom, why did that officer pull us over?" Luke asked.

"Mom, I am kind of scared," Hope said.

"I am not sure why, Luke," Lucy told him, "but don't be scared guys. Everything is just fine. We have done nothing wrong, after all."

Several minutes passed, and the officer returned. "Please step out of the car, ma'am." Lucy unbuckled her seat belt and climbed out of the car. "Is something wrong officer?"

"Miss Meriweather, have you been drinking this evening?"

"No, no, of course not."

"Well, I am going to have to do a sobriety test to determine that." The officer sneered. He was looking at Lucy like she was a criminal. He went through a series of tests with Lucy, including asking her to walk a straight line. She complied silently, getting more worried by the minute. Next the officer said, "Miss Meriweather, I am going to need to search your car. Please get your children out of the car and wait over here."

"Search my car for what?" Lucy demanded.

"I don't need to answer to you, ma'am. Now please, get your kids, and wait over there." His voice was forceful, bordering on angry.

Lucy quickly gathered up her kids and her purse. Hope was crying and clutching Lucy tightly. Even Luke looked at his mother with wide eyes, holding her hand tightly. The officer proceeded to ransack her car, emptying the glove box, the trunk, and then taking Lucy's purse and dumping the contents out on the hood of the car. He opened the small amber bottle of essential oils that Lucy kept in her purse for bug bites.

"What is this?" He demanded, smelling it. "Drugs?"

"Of course not." Lucy said incredulously. "It is a blend of plant oils. I put it on insect bites."

"Sure it is." He sneered, dumping the contents out on the ground.

"Well, miss, I did not find anything this time, so you are free to go. Just let it be known that we know who you are, and we are watching you."

"What do you mean, this time? What were you looking for?"

But the officer just climbed back in his car and pulled away, leaving Lucy and her kids to clean up the mess he had made of their car. Lucy was so angry she was shaking. The policeman was just harassing her, and she knew that she would not have any luck making a complaint. She and the kids got back in the car and drove home in silence. She considered calling Doug to tell him about her experience, but decided against it. After all, she was trying to stay positive.

After the kids were in bed, Lucy opened her laptop to send out an energy request to all of her Reiki friends.

Dear friends,

It seems that I have come to a point in my life where I am being persecuted for my beliefs. The small town that I have moved to, Rocky Point, Colorado, has discovered that I am a practicing witch. The towns people have been grossly misinformed about my craft. There is a lot of fear and unsettled energy in Rocky Point tonight. I have worked hard to sow seeds of love with my neighbors for the time that I have lived here. I have faith that my efforts will pay off in the end. I am prompted to remember the 3 fold rule, that all good that I do will be returned to me 3 fold. It is for this reason that I have chose not to fight back. I am unwilling to attract 3 times the negativity that I would be sending out!

I am writing to all of you to request your good energy and love. I would like everyone to send Reiki to Rocky Point and all of the people living here, that their fears will be put to rest. Please send love and light to my home and my family as well. My children are noticing the effects of the fear and hatred that has been sown here recently.

Thank you all for your efforts, I am certain that we will be able to reverse this unhappy situation!

Namaste,

Lucy

She had just sent her email when she noticed bright light in the front yard. She ran to the window to discover that her lawn was on fire. A giant fiery cross lit up her front yard. Lucy cried out in disbelief, raced down the stairs and out the front door. A startled teenager in the yard looked her in the eye, then jumped on his motorcycle and sped out of her driveway. Lucy could see the fear in his eyes when he looked at her. She could feel his heart racing as he disappeared down the road. He was a neighborhood kid, she was sure.

The flaming cross in the yard was putting off a lot of heat. Acrid fumes burned her nose and lungs. The fire was very close to her flower beds and an ancient Weeping Willow tree, whose long fingers stretched nearly to the ground. Lucy ran to the side of the house and turned the spigot on, and charged toward the fire with the end of the hose. The water collided with fire, making a hiss and plume of steam and smoke that hung heavy in the air. She continued watering down the grass for several minutes, until no more smoke rose from the ashes where a thick carpet of green grass used to lay.

After dousing the fire, Lucy curled up on the porch swing and sobbed. She knew that it would only make things worse to call the police. She did not want to wake Doug either. Finally, she did the best thing she knew to do. She called on the God and Goddess to protect her family and soothe her aching heart. Finally she went to bed, feeling much more peaceful and safe.

chapter 11

THREE DOORS DOWN, someone else was feeling uneasy. Jason Jones had crept back into the house from his late night adventure, and gone straight to his room. Being the pastor's son had its drawbacks. Jason was always privy to the drama going around town. Since his mother had seen the neighbor, Lucy, on Book TV, no one could talk about anything else. Especially his father. The pastor had been on the phone with the police, the congregation, and colleagues nonstop.

From what Jason had gathered, Lucy was a practicing witch. His father believed that she was deep into devil worship, and had been planning to do something evil to the town. She had started by charming a local widower, Doug Brown, into falling in love with her. The pastor figured that she would try to lead Doug, his children and his family onto a wayward path that would turn them into evil beings. From there, they would continue to branch out until the whole town had been turned. Earlier that day, Jason overheard a conversation between his father and the chief of police, who had stopped by to talk.

"I am telling you, Dan, we have to do something!" Pastor Jones insisted.

"I know what you are saying Pastor, but technically she has not broken any laws."

"Did you complete that background check?"

"Yup, we sure did. It came back clean. She has never even had a speeding ticket. That doesn't mean that she does not have aliases, though."

"Can't you check for that?"

"Not really. If we had any evidence that she had committed any crimes, we could run her prints and picture through a national database in Denver. So far, though, we have got nothing."

"Can't you search her house for drugs or something?" The pastor was sounding desperate.

"Not without cause, but maybe we could search her car. If one of my guys pulled her over, he could find some reason to justify a search. Maybe we would find something then." The Sheriff sat back in his chair, hands clasped behind his head.

"Okay, great. Let me know as soon as you find something. I need something to take back to the Browns to show them that she is not as innocent as they think she is." The pastor rose and shook the sheriff's hand.

This whole thing is so crazy, Jason thought. We just need to find a way to run Lucy out of town, and this whole mess would be done with. That is when he came up with a plan. If I can just scare her enough, surely she will leave. He had waited until his parents were asleep, grabbed some matches from the kitchen, and strapped a full gas can to his motorbike. He rolled his bike down the driveway, and headed to Lucy's house. It was easy to decide on a cross. After all, wouldn't the mark of Christ be a horrible thing for the witch to look out on everyday? He carefully poured the gas onto the grass in the image of a giant cross. When he threw a lit match onto the grass, he leapt back, startled. The crossed flamed up with a loud "Whoosh!" For a second he was afraid that the house would start on fire. He felt glued to the spot where he stood, afraid of what he had just done. Suddenly, the front door flew open and Lucy appeared on the steps. She looked Jason right in the eye. Terrified, he jumped on his motorbike and took off as fast as he could. He went straight home, stripped off his gas soaked clothes, and got into his bed. He knew that Lucy had seen his face, but did she know who he is? Many questions rolled about in Jason's head. Would she call the police? What if his father found out? Would he be the town hero, or would he be in trouble? Suddenly, Jason realized that he may have bigger problems. What if Lucy really was as dangerous as his father thought that she was? Could she put a curse on him, or hex him or something? Could she kill him? Jason felt sick inside. Why did I do something so stupid, he wondered. Finally, he drifted off to an uneasy sleep, full of worries and fears.

The next morning Lucy walked out front to assess the damage. The cross was seared deep into the grass. The burn was at least fifteen feet long by ten feet wide. The long, feathery tips of the Weeping Willow were black and singed. Lucy's heart hurt for the beautiful old tree. The flowers nearest the flames were curled back and burned as well. She found a gas can and a box of matches in the driveway that her late night visitor must had dropped in his haste. She fought back the urge to sit in the middle of the charred mess and cry. Instead, Lucy sat down, cross legged amongst the destroyed yard and meditated. She called in Elementals like Faeries and Gnomes to watch over and heal the damaged foliage. She felt peace wash over her, and she knew that her yard would recover. She asked, again, for universal energy to sweep into her yard and clear the negative vibes that existed there from the vicious attack. Afterward, Lucy fed her children breakfast, did some laundry, and watched a movie with Hope. She was determined to keep things normal at home for her children. They did not deserve to be frightened by all of this. When Luke asked her what happened to the lawn, she downplayed it and said that she was not sure.

After lunch, Megan called.

"Lucy, I just read your email. What the hell is going on?" Megan thought of Lucy like a sister, and was ready to stand up and fight if anyone messed with her.

"Well, someone saw my Book TV spot, and now the whole town is convinced that I am some sort of evil in their town. No big deal."

"No big deal? Like hell, no big deal! Are you okay? Has anyone tried to hurt you?"

"Well, no, not really. I got pulled over last night and searched. I was never really sure why, though."

"Lucy, that is illegal. They can't pull you over for no reason and harass you! You need to file a complaint!" Megan was nearly yelling into the phone.

"No way, that is the opposite of the way I want to handle this. I am determined to stay positive."

"Really? I can't see how you are not power pissed. I am. Has anything else happened?" Megan was pacing around her apartment.

"Well, yeah, but I don't know if I should tell you. You are already mad, and you have not heard the worst of it yet." Lucy was well aware of Megan's temper.

Megan took a deep breath. "It's okay, I can deal with it. Tell me."

Lucy proceeded to tell her all about the cross in the yard, and what she had done about it.

"Oh my god, Lucy. I am so sorry. This is terrible." Megan sounded shaken. "You don't even dare call the police, do you?"

"No, I don't. I think that it would make things worse, don't you?"

"Maybe. But did you say that you know the kid who did it?"

"No, I'm not sure. He looked so scared when I saw him. I wonder how he is feeling now."

"It hope he is scared shitless, the little bastard."

"Megan!"

"Sorry, but I am having a hard time finding anything positive about this situation. You are not safe there! Why don't you come back to Denver for a while? I am sure Tina would love to have you."

"Nope, I can't do that. I am not leaving Doug here to deal with this alone. Besides, I love my house and my garden. I am not leaving."

"Please, Lucy. I am begging you. Just for a little while? Until it is safer?" Megan pleaded.

"Not gonna happen Meg. I appreciate your support, I really do. But running away is not going to solve this. Not only that, I have to think about my kids. They need to feel safe, and hiding out at Tina's would scare the heck out of them. Please, send the Reiki. Help me deal with this my way."

"Okay," Megan resigned. "I will. What are you planning?"

"I am going to do a candle spell this evening to spread love throughout the town. So far, that is my plan."

"I have a spell you can do for your Pastor and your arsonist neighbor," Megan said sarcastically. "It goes something like this: *Each time your tongue recites my name, Each time your ugly thoughts defame, Your tongue and mind shall feel the pain, of pricking needles and fiery flame.*"

"Megan!" Lucy laughed. "Honestly, do you really want that pain sent back to you, threefold?"

In the evening, Lucy put together a plan for her spell. Since her goal was to spread love and peace in Rocky Point, she selected a light blue candle, for peace and unity. Lucy cast a circle around her altar. She called in the goddess Kuan Yin to assist her in her work. Kuan Yin is a goddess who promotes peace among people and has no enemies. She lit a bit of rose petal incense, and began her ritual. Using her athame, Lucy carved Rocky Point into the side of the candle, then anointed it with basil oil for harmony, and rose oil for love. As she lit the candle, she chanted, *"I call upon the powers of Light, to fill this town with love tonight. Cast out darkness, lies, and fear, leave only peace and kindness here."* She continued the chant until she had repeated it three times, then settled in to meditate with the candle as it burned down.

Doug's day was not peaceful either. He finally deleted his entire voice mail box after the tenth message from congregation members. They were pretty much all the same thing anyway. *"Hi Doug, this is so and so. I understand that you are going through a pretty tough time right now. I just wanted to let you know that you are in my family's thoughts and prayers. If there is anything we can do for you, anything at all, please let me know."*

How ironic, Doug thought, that my happiness makes people think that I am 'struggling', or 'going through a tough time', or 'needing some extra support'. And yet, it was nice that people cared. They were doing what they thought was right, Doug knew. After all, most people are just listening to the rumors that being spread around, and they believed what they are hearing.

Doug was in the shower, when Brian knocked on the door. "Dad, Uncle David and Uncle Brandon are here. They said that they need to talk to you."

Doug sighed. "Alright son. Tell them they can go sit out on the deck and I will be out in a few minutes."

When Doug joined the men on the patio, they all greeted him with somber expressions. "Hi guys, what's up?"

"What's up?" Brandon snapped. "Seriously, Doug. You know dang well why we are here."

"Do I?" Doug countered. "Are you here to exorcise me? Or perhaps to tell me that I have to break things off with Lucy? Please, tell me why you are here!" Doug's voice was a little louder than he meant it to be. He realized that he sounded very defensive.

"Careful Brandon," David said quietly. "The pastor warned you not to upset him."

"What?! Not to upset me, why?" Doug was really getting irritated. "What do you think will happen?"

"Nobody thinks anything will happen Doug," David said, putting his arm on Doug's shoulder. "We are just really worried about you, that's all."

Doug threw his head back and sighed. "Look, I know that you guys think that something terrible is going on with Lucy and me, but you are wrong."

"Okay, can we just sit down and talk then," Brandon said, sitting down on a deck chair.

"As you know," David began, "It has come to our attention that you have not been very forthcoming with us about Lucy's religion."

"I guess I did not think that Lucy's religion was any of your business," Doug snapped. "If she were Christian, none of you would even care, would you?"

"But she is not Christian, Doug," David reminded him. "That is the problem. She is into some dark, dangerous stuff."

"We just don't want to see you get hurt," Brandon said, softening his tone. "You have been through enough already without this."

"Look, Lucy may not be who you thought she was, but I love her, and that has not changed."

"How can you say that?" Brandon demanded. "How can you sit here and say that you love a witch! A servant to Satan!"

"Argh!" Doug groaned. "Listen to yourself! How stupid do you think I am? Don't you think that I am aware of what Lucy is and is not?"

"I used to think so, but now," David shrugged, "who knows."

"We just need to hear it from you, Doug. We need to hear what you know about Lucy. Dad thinks that we are all overreacting. Mom wants to believe in Lucy. We are just worried." Brandon shook his head. "You have no idea the stories we have been hearing."

"Okay, look, when I first met Lucy, I was drawn to her. There is just something about her, you know?" Doug gazed off dreamily. "She made me feel things I have not felt in a very long time."

"Yeah, I can see that," Brandon nodded.

"After I realized I was having feelings for her, I googled her. She said she was a New Age author, and I wondered what that was. The biography that I found spelled it out to me. Lucy Meriweather. Practicing Wiccan. Did you know that her mother is the High Priestess of her coven?"

"No, Doug," David replied sarcastically. "How in the world would we know that?"

"Oh, true. Well anyway, she is. And she is a very nice person." Doug stood up and leaned against the railing of the deck. "I decided that I could not date her, and I tried to avoid her. Every time I turned around, though, there she was. Finally, we ended up at her house for dinner. She has this amazing house, by the way."

"That is a cool old house," Brandon said, softening. "What happened while you were there?"

"She sat me down and told me that she was Wiccan, and explained to me what that meant. I asked her a lot of questions. The funny thing is, everyone is freaking out that she is a devil worshiper or something, but Wiccans don't even believe in the Devil. There is no devil or hell in her belief system."

"Are you sure?" David asked skeptically. "That is not what the pastor is saying."

"Yes, I am sure. I have done my fair share of reading the last few weeks. It is true. No devil. No evil worshiping or sacrificing of kittens, either."

"So what does this all mean, Doug," Brandon asked. "Are you leaving the church? Are you planning on become a wizard?"

"Really?" Doug asked, laughing. "A wizard? This is not Harry Potter, you know."

Brandon flushed red. "I don't know what to call it. One of them, I mean."

"No, I am happy with my faith. I don't think Lucy would hear of it anyway. She is always encouraging me to go to church."

"That seems weird to me," David admitted. "Why would she want to encourage a religion that she doesn't even believe in?"

"Because she knows that my church is important to me. She even asked me to pray about our current situation. She thinks that if we spread love, that eventually, the people in Rocky Point will settle down and be more accepting." Doug was relieved to see that his brothers were open to listening to reason. "That is just how she is. She is accepting of all people, regardless of their religion, race, sexual preference, and so on."

"Well, so are we," Brandon insisted.

"Really? Then why the witch hunt?" Doug asked. "Sometimes I think that Lucy is more Christ like that most of the Christians I know."

Brandon stared at the floor. No one spoke for a couple of minutes. Finally, he broke the silence. "Point taken brother. I feel really stupid about all of this. We have been gossiping and spreading lies about Lucy. She does not deserve this."

"I know," David agreed. "I am feeling pretty rotten too. Sorry we doubted you Doug."

Doug shrugged. "It is good to have family who cares. Lucy thinks that I should be flattered by all of the hubbub. You know, that people care enough about me to be worried."

"From here on out, you can count on us to be on your side. We will not buy into any more foolishness." Brandon reached out and shook Doug's hand. David followed suit.

After his brothers had left, Doug sat out on the deck thinking for a long time. He was surprised that things had gone so well with this family. Could it be, he wondered, that his prayer worked? Perhaps. Then again, maybe whatever spell work or energy work that Lucy was doing had worked. Either way, he was grateful.

☙❧

Sunday morning arrived, presenting Doug with a real challenge. If he went to church, he would be dealing with a lot of issues. If he stayed home, he would be the focus of even more speculation. Finally, he called Lucy.

"Hello, beautiful. Did I wake you?"

"Hi Doug! I miss you! And no, you did not wake me. I was working on my new book."

"Oh, sorry to disturb you then. Do you have time to talk?"

"Sure, what's up? Shouldn't you be getting ready for church?"

"I am ready to go. I am just trying really hard to talk myself out of going. That's why I called. What do you think I should do?"

"Why would you miss church Doug? Are you sick?" Lucy asked innocently.

"No, I am not sick! You know dang well why I don't want to go."

"Oh, do you mean because of the trouble while we were gone?"

Doug sighed, wondering why Lucy insisted on playing these games. "Of course that is what I mean. How can you even wonder?"

Lucy laughed. "Oh, Doug, don't get all frustrated. You have prayed. I have worked my magic. In my mind, the whole thing is over. Time to get on with our lives, right?"

"Well, sure, if it was that easy. You don't understand what it will be like at church though. People will be staring at me, whispering. Acting all concerned. I just don't know how to handle all of that."

"Doug, let me ask you something. Have you done anything wrong?"

"No, I haven't. Nothing at all."

"Have you worshiped false idols? Consorted with Satan anytime lately? Anything like that?" Lucy giggled.

"No," Doug laughed too. "Not that I can think of, anyway."

"Then please, stop acting so freaking guilty. You are innocent. I am innocent. There is no reason to slink around trying to avoid anybody. Just go to church, do what you always do, and then come and see me, okay?"

"Okay, I think I can do that."

"Good. Now hurry up. I miss you!"

Fifteen minutes later, Doug and the kids pulled into the parking lot at the church. When they were walking in, a group teenagers stood near the door talking quietly and staring at them. "What?" Doug asked, brushing his nose with the back of his hand "Do I have a booger? Did I get it?" The teens turned red and laughed.

"Doug, honey, I am so glad that you came," Cheryl whispered as they joined the rest of the Browns on the pew. "I am feeling good that this is going to blow over in no time!"

It came as no surprise to Doug that the service was all about avoiding the temptations of Satan. The pastor kept trying to meet his eye while he was giving his sermon. Doug finally gave in and looked at the pastor with big, innocent eyes. He held his gaze firmly for several seconds, until the pastor looked away. After the service, Doug ushered his children quickly to the car, hoping to avoid any more awkward glances.

When Doug pulled into Lucy's driveway, he was shocked to see that her front yard had a huge black burned spot. He climbed out of his car and walked over to get a closer look. When he realized that he was looking at a giant cross he gasped.

"Pretty ugly, isn't it?" Lucy asked, walking up behind him.

"What happened?" Doug was livid, tense with anger.

"Someone wanted to make a statement, that's all." Lucy took him by the hand and led him to the porch swing.

"When?" Doug growled.

"Around two in the morning, the night we got home."

"WHY didn't you call me?" Doug demanded hotly.

"Because I knew that you would be really upset. Like you are now."

"Of course I am upset! This is a horrible thing to do. Whoever did it is going to answer to me!" Doug felt like his head was going to explode.

Lucy had never seen Doug get angry like this. He was red faced and tense. "I know how bad it is. I was on my laptop when my bedroom lit up like it was daytime. I got the hose on it as fast as I could, but it still burned clear to the soil," Lucy said sadly. "Some of my flowers and trees were damaged too."

"That must have been really scary Lucy," Doug said, calming down a little bit. "I know how much you love your yard. Did you call the police?"

"Well, no." Oh crap, Lucy thought. Now I am going to have to tell him about getting pulled over.

"Why?" Doug asked incredulously. "You cannot just let this go! This is vandalism. What if your house had caught fire?"

"I am afraid that the police are not really on my side. Try not to get too mad, but there is something else that I have not told you...." And she told him all about getting pulled over. By the end of her story Doug was standing, pacing around the porch like he did not know which way to turn.

"How dare they!" Doug exploded. "How dare they target you! You have done nothing! Nothing to deserve this treatment!"

"Doug, please come and sit with me," Lucy implored quietly. "I want to teach you something."

Doug sat stiffly next to Lucy, still too angry to settle down. "One principal that I operate by is the Law of Attraction. The Law of Attraction is a universal law that teaches us that what we think about most, we attract into our lives. If we stay positive and optimistic, we attract the very best thing. If we allow ourselves to be negative and unhappy, we will attract more of the same. I think that now is a really good time to put the Law of Attraction to work for us."

"So what you are saying is that if we are mad and combative with Rocky Point, we will get more of it back? It seems like they are doing it anyway, no matter what we do."

"Yes, I am saying that. Honestly Doug, we may have attracted this to ourselves in the first place. We were both wrapped up in the idea that if people figured out who I am, then they would freak out. Right?"

"Yeah, so?"

"So, we asked for it, and we got it. Now we need to fix it. We need to think only loving thoughts of our neighbors and expect this to all blow over very soon. We need to expect that we are surrounded by loving people who will accept our differences and allow us to be happy."

"I really have a hard time believing that we deserved this, or that we caused it." Doug shook his head. "I would never, ever ask for you to be harassed by the police or nearly have your house burned down."

"I know, it seems pretty extreme right now. Humor me though, okay? Help me to stay positive and let this work itself out as it should. We can do this together."

Doug finally agreed, unable to say no to Lucy.

chapter 12

THE NEXT MORNING Lucy drove into Denver to run some errands. On the way back home, she stopped at the gas station. When she walked inside to pay for her gas there was a commotion going on at the counter. A teenager was pleading with the counter attendant.

"Please don't call the police, I must have forgotten my wallet at home. I am not trying to steal gas."

The greasy haired man at the counter shook his head and picked up the phone. "You can tell that to the cops. We have had way too much theft around here lately."

"Excuse me," Lucy intervened. "What is going on here? Maybe I can help."

The surly man turned to Lucy. "This punk kid put gas in his motorcycle then came in here and said that he ain't got no money. I have to call the cops when people steal gas."

"But I told you," the boy said, "I am not a thief. I made an honest mistake."

"Tell you what," Lucy told the attendant. "I will pay for his gas and you can put your phone away." Lucy swiped her card and paid for the gas. As she walked to her car, the teenager stopped her. When Lucy turned around to face him, the blood ran out of the boys face.

"Thank you for helping me out," he stammered, looking shocked. Then he jumped on his motorcycle and raced out of the parking lot without looking back.

Lucy thought that his behavior was very strange but did not understand why until early the next morning. She was just pouring a cup of coffee when she heard something in the front yard. When she went to the window, Lucy was surprised to see the same boy from the gas station digging up the charred grass on her front yard.

Jason, on the other hand, had been very surprised when Lucy had saved him at the gas station. He knew that Lucy would not recognize him but he was amazed that she would help someone that she didn't even know. After he left the gas station he thought a lot about what he had done to Lucy's lawn. In the beginning he thought that Lucy was evil, and that she deserved to pay. Obviously Lucy was not evil at all. Jason had laid in bed all night wondering what to do. He knew that he needed to make things right. He got up early and slipped out the front door before anyone else was awake. Now he was working hard to dig out the ruined parts of the lawn so that he could fix his mistake.

Lucy walked outside and sat down on the porch swing with her coffee. Jason was working so hard that he did not notice her. After watching Jason for a little while, Lucy spoke, "Why don't you take a break and visit with me for a few minutes?"

Jason was startled out of his thoughts. Hanging his head, he approached the steps. "I was kind of hoping to get this done before you woke up. I am so sorry."

Lucy motioned for Jason to sit down. "I am really very confused. Who are you, and why did you do this?"

"My name is Jason, ma'am. I am the pastor's son. All of this talk of a witch and devil worshipers got me all riled up I guess. I just wanted to make a statement. I just meant to scare you a little but the fire was much bigger than I had planned."

"You do realize," Lucy said, "that you could have burned my house down with me and my innocent children inside."

"Yes," Jason wept. "It was so stupid and I feel so bad. Then to make it even worse you saved me yesterday. I think that guy was really going to call the police. My dad would have killed me."

"Well," Lucy said, sipping her coffee, "that was no big deal. Anyone would have done the same thing."

"No ma'am," Luke argued. "There were several other people who came in and no one offered to help me but you. I guess what I want to know is if you are so bad why would you help out a perfect stranger? I have been trying to figure that out all night. The answer as far as I can tell is that you are not bad. I really need to make up for my mistakes here."

"I really appreciate your honesty Jason. I know that I have made mistakes in my life as well. It takes a big person to own up and fix it. Why don't you keep on working for a while and I will fix breakfast." Lucy went inside and made pancakes and fruit. When the table was set, she sent Hope out to get Jason.

Jason washed his hands at the sink and joined Lucy and the kids at the table. "It is really nice of you to feed me. You really didn't have to do that," Jason commented between mouthfuls of pancakes.

"No biggie Jason," Lucy smiled. "I am really glad that we had this chance to get to know other."

By early afternoon, the charred grass had been removed and new soil was in its place. Jason and the kids raked grass seed into the soil. Jason was surprised by how much he enjoyed being around Lucy and her children. They had been laughing and playing all day. "This is such a happy place to be," he mused. He apologized to Lucy one more time before he headed home.

"I am not mad at you Jason. I just want you to learn from this situation. Things are not always as they seem. Take time to get to know someone before you judge them or you might miss out on an opportunity to make a new friend." Lucy hugged Jason and he got on his bike and went home.

Later in the day Doug and his children came over to roast hot dogs. Doug was surprised to see that Lucy had finished fixing her grass. He was even more surprised to hear the story of how the grass was fixed.

"Jason Jones, huh? I guess that I could have guessed that one, but still...I hate to think that anyone in this town is capable of doing something so destructive."

"What do you mean, you could have guessed that one?"

"You know, Pastor's kid syndrome. Always trying to live up to his dad. And the Pastor is not what you might call easy to deal with. I suppose Jason is constantly trying to win his dad's approval."

"Wow, that hadn't occurred to me. He is actually a great kid, arson aside." Lucy felt bad to think that Jason was trying so hard to gain some recognition from his dad. "Not many teenagers would have come back over here and fixed their mistake, you know?"

"True, that took a lot of courage."

"You know, I think that I am going to have to take a page out of Jason's book. If he can face me, I think that I can face his dad."

Doug sucked in his breath. "Ouch. Are you sure about that? Who knows what he may say to you. I'm not sure that this is a good idea Lucy."

"Look Doug, Pastor Jones is the root of the issue here in Rocky Point. If I can win him over, we will be in much better shape." Lucy had made up her mind. She walked into the house, put on shoes and a sweater and walked to the Pastors house.

Jason was laying on his bed, reading an article on his laptop when someone rang the doorbell. Suddenly, he heard the angry voice of his father.

"What do you think you are doing here? Haven't you done enough damage? Leave at once or I will call the police and have you arrested for trespassing!"

Jason crept to the top to stairs to see what was going on. His heat sank when he saw Lucy at the door, trying to speak to his father.

"That is not necessary Pastor. I just wanted to speak with you for a few minutes. Can we please talk?" Lucy remained calm and did her best to smile and send love to the angry man.

"Talk about what? No, I don't need to hear anymore lies from you. Get out of here and stay away from my family!" With that he slammed the door in Lucy's face and stormed into his office.

Lucy look stunned for a moment, Jason wondered if she was on the verge of tears. Instead, she placed both hands flat on the front door, closed her eyes and spoke softly. Jason could not hear her words, but a deep sense of peace and love washed over him. Her invocation sounded like this, *"Love and light, banish fear. Leave only peace and forgiveness here."*

When Lucy walked up her driveway, she was surprised to see three extra cars at her house. She spotted Doug sitting on the porch with his parents, brothers and sisters in law. She softly repeated the same invocation again and again, as she neared the house. *"Love and light, banish fear. Leave only peace and forgiveness here."*

Doug met her halfway through the yard. "I did not know they were coming. They said that they need to say something to you. Sorry."

"Don't be sorry. I need to speak with them as well. I'm glad that they are here." Lucy was still a little shaken from the encounter with the pastor, but she was relieved to see Doug's family. Come what may, we need to talk this out, she knew.

"Hi everyone," she smiled, joining Doug on the swing. "What a mess Doug and I have created, huh?"

"No, dear," Cheryl began. "What a mess we have all created. I hope that you can forgive us for intruding today, but we need to tell you how sorry we all are that we have gotten mixed up in the drama."

"I am the one who should be sorry." Doug tried to protest but Lucy put her hand gently on his mouth and continued. "I was raised to love everyone. I try to live my life in a way that attracts more love and happiness to me. This time I let my own fear of being different rule my actions. Due to that, I have attracted a lot of fear from others. The responsibility is mine."

"I can't let you take all of the blame," Doug insisted. "I felt like I had to hide your true essence from my family instead of having the courage to stand up for you. I should have handled this differently too."

"Well, while we are blaming ourselves," David smiled, "Be sure to lay some on me. I got caught up in drama and foolishness. I have always liked you Lucy. I can't believe I allowed myself to get so wound up."

"Me too," Liz added. "I guess we all played a role here. If it wasn't for Bob making us listen to reason, we might all still be misinformed and angry."

"Lucy, Doug told us about the fire and being pulled over. We are just sick about that." Cheryl's eyed filled with tears. "What can we do to help?"

"Well, there is one thing that might help." Lucy told them about her plan to do their own spiritual work to help make things better. "I know that it may seem odd, combining forces, but I have faith in my work, as I know that you have faith in yours. Can we work together to spread love all around Rocky Point? Hate cannot exist where love is shining brightly."

"Let me get this straight, you want us to pray for all of the people in town who have been attacking you and Doug? You want us to love them?" Brandon was not sure he could do that.

"Exactly. If we get angry and spread hate, we just attract more of the same. Instead, let's choose to love these guys, regardless of their behavior."

"In our church, we have faith in Jesus Christ," Bob spoke up. "Jesus loved everyone, not just those who looked, felt or acted like him. He didn't ask us to be nice to people we like, he asked us to love everyone. Period."

"I know all of that," Nicole said frowning, "And I will certainly pray. I just think that we have to go farther than that. We have to support Lucy and Doug in a more public way. Maybe when our friends and congregation members see us acting like a normal, loving family, they will feel more at ease."

The family all nodded in agreement, making plans to spend more time together publicly. Lucy was so touched that they were willing to rally around her and Doug. Plans were made to have dinner at the local diner the following evening. As the Browns left, many hugs were exchanged.

"Doug, you truly have an amazing family." Lucy remarked as the last car left the driveway.

"I know, I have been so fortunate to be a part of them. With them, you and our kids, I feel like the luckiest guy in the world."

"Our kids. I have to say, I like the sound of that a lot." Lucy pulled Doug into a long, lingering kiss.

"Wait a second," Doug exclaimed. "I forgot all about your talk with the Pastor. How did it go?"

Lucy twirled her long hair around her finger, finding the best words to use. "Lets just say that I need to love him more before I try to talk to him again."

166

"Seriously? Was it that bad?"

"Brutal. But remember, love attracts love. We will keep loving him. Eventually, he will be ready."

☜☞

Jason Jones sat on at the top of stairs for a long while. He had never seen his father so angry before. He was tough to please, there was no doubt about that, but to threaten the police. That was serious. Jason knew that Lucy was a wonderful person. He knew that she deserved to be respected. If only his dad could see past their differences, perhaps he would see that too, Jason mused. Suddenly, he had an idea. He returned to his room, printed the article he had been reading on his laptop, and walked downstairs to his dad's office. The Pastor was pacing next to the window.

Jason took a deep breath. "Dad, I need to talk to you."

"Can this wait? I have a lot of my mind right now."

"No dad, it can't. You always say that. I need to talk to you now and it is important to me."

Tim Jones turned at looked at his son, sighing. "Fine, what do you need?"

As Tim settled into his burgundy office chair, Jason sat down across from the desk in a soft armchair. "Dad, I need to tell you some things, and I don't want you to get mad and yell at me until I am all done, okay?"

Tim rested his elbows on his desk and looked at Jason expectantly. Jason was a good kid, but was not free from his own sins. Recently he had been arrested for shoplifting. The Pastor had convinced the store owners not to press charges, but he promised Jason that if he ever did something like that again he would be dealt with severely. Lately he had been sullen, moody and spent most of his time in his bedroom.

"Alright, I won't yell. What do you need to tell me?"

"I burned a cross in Lucy's yard. A huge flaming cross on her grass. I nearly set her house on fire. It was horrible. She was scared nearly to death and so was I. After all I heard you saying about her at home, I just wanted to scare her, you know? She just put it out with the hose, cried on her front steps, and went to bed. She didn't call the police. She didn't even try to catch me."

"JASON! What the hell were you thinking?" Tim bellowed, his face turning red.

"Wait, there is more. You promised to listen." Jason took a deep breath, his hands shaking. "The next day, I rode my motorbike into Denver. I wanted to do some shopping for mom's birthday. When I got to town, I stopped for gas. I filled up my bike and walked inside to pay. That is when I realized that I had left my wallet at home. The store clerk got really mad. He called me a thief and a liar. I tried to call you to pay on your credit card but your receptionist said that you were busy with church business and couldn't talk. The store said that they were going to call the police and have me arrested. People were staring at me, giving me dirty looks. They believed that I was really a criminal. A thief."

Tim's face had softened a little, but he was still clenching his jaw tightly. "Go on."

"Just as the clerk was dialing the phone, a woman walked in and asked what the problem was. The clerk told her that I was stealing gas and he was calling the police. She immediately pulled out her debit card and paid my bill. I stopped her in the parking lot to thank her. When she turned around, I felt like I had been punched in the stomach. The lady who saved me was Lucy Meriweather, dad." Tears were running freely down Jason's face. "After the horrible thing that I did to her, she kept me from being arrested. She didn't even know who I was, either. She was saving a stranger for no reason. She said it was no problem, that it is our job to help each other out from time to time."

Tim blew out long stream of air. "This is serious Jason. You have caused a lot of trouble for me."

"I'm still not done dad. You know what though? This is about me, not you." Jason blew his nose and continued. "I came back home feeling terrible. I knew that I had to make up for what I had done. I got up really early this morning and went back to Lucy's house to survey the damage. I decided that the cross would have to be dug out, soil replaced, and grass replanted. I got starting digging out the charred ruined mess. I was hoping to get it done quickly before she even woke up but it took a lot longer than I thought. I was only halfway done digging when I realized that she was sitting on the steps watching me. She was so nice to me, dad! She fixed me breakfast. Eventually, she and her kids pitched in to get the job finished. It was hard work, too. She even told me that she wasn't mad at me, but she hoped I had learned something about judging people."

Jason stood up and walked to the window. He watched some finches flitting in and out of a feeder hanging outside. "You say that she is so bad, but she isn't. You say that she is evil, but that isn't true. You say that we are supposed to love everyone, but you don't! You don't know anything about her and yet you tell people terrible things!" Jason was shouting now, rage roaring in his ears. "She came over here to talk to you and you treated her like dirt. Worse than dirt. Like a criminal! Why would you do that?"

"Jason, please sit down. You asked me to allow you to speak, and I did. Now give me the same respect."

Jason slumped down in the arm chair, new tears, furious tears slipping down his face. He had never confronted his father that way before. He was frightened and proud of himself, all at the same time.

"First of all, the fire was a really stupid thing to do, but I guess you already know that. I am very grateful that Lucy saved you from being arrested. You must have been so scared. I know that I would have been. It took a big man to go to her house and try to fix your mistake, especially after the things you had heard about Lucy." Tim looked at his watch, frowning. "I have a meeting at the church in just a few minutes. Can we talk more about this more later?"

"Yeah, but dad, before you leave, take this with you. You need to read it." Jason thrust the article that he had printed from the internet into his dad's hands and returned to his room.

chapter 13

"HI MARIE," PASTOR Jones greeted his secretary as he entered the church office.

"Hi Pastor. Your next appointment canceled. You have an hour before the board meeting."

Tim walked into his office and settled down at his desk. His conversation with Jason was still hanging heavily on his mind. His relationship with his son had been strained for awhile now. Sometimes he felt like he could not be an adequate father with the responsibilities of his church. Curiosity led him to pull the folded papers out of his pocket that Jason had asked him to read.

"Which Witch is Which?"

In these modern days, more and more interpretations of religion are popping up. The church of Wicca, which is often confused with Paganism, is currently gaining a lot of attention. For one to understand Wicca, they must first understand Paganism. There are many misnomers about Pagan beliefs that are incorrect. The early Christian church is often blamed for the bad information. The early leaders of the Catholic church certainly may have played a role.

Paganism is a term used to describe all non-Christian religions. Paganism is ancient and has many different types; Druids, Celtics, even Aboriginal tribes in New Zealand and Hindus - all Pagan. The most common falsehood about Paganism is that it is in any way associated with devil worship. The devil, or Satan, is a Christian character. Pagan religions do not even have a belief in hell or Satan.

Wicca is a fairly new religion that falls under the umbrella of Paganism. Wicca is a coven based religion that recognizes the Goddess and God. Covens are groups of people practicing their religion together, similar to a congregation. It is difficult to nail down specific beliefs and practices because most covens have their own ideas, rituals and creed. Some covens practice sexual fertility rites and some do not. Wicca tends to be more open to interpretation than most Christian religions. Many Wiccans also have some belief in other theology as well.

Lucy Meriweather, author of "Why We are Wiccan", explains her philosophy beautifully.

"People often ask me why I walk the path of a witch. It is an easy answer for me. I want to spread love. I want to spread peace and understanding. Wicca gives me the freedom to follow my own intuition. I recognize that I am a powerful, divine being, a Goddess in my own right. If more human beings understood their own vast potential to spread love and make the world a better place, can you imagine how wonderful it would be? I firmly believe that by loving instead of fearing, I can make a difference in this world. My love, my actions, and my example can encourage people of all faiths to be the best that they can be. I don't expect anyone to join me on my path, it is mine alone to follow. It is my responsibility to inspire every person that I come in contact with to walk their own path with love, compassion, and understanding. Sometimes I am misunderstood. Sometimes there are people who are stuck in fear who cannot see past our differences. That just encourages me to love more, understand more, and spread more light."

The article continued, but the Pastor kept going back over Lucy's words. Spread love, light, encourage...all of the things she had been doing in Rocky Point. Until he had smeared her reputation all over town that is. Stuck in fear. Yeah, that described him really well. Not following his own doctrine, really. Just operating through fear and drama. It was hard for Tim to admit when he was wrong. Really hard. He knew that he had to do something to fix this, but what? Deep shame enveloped him when he thought about the way he treated Lucy earlier that day. Her words continued to echo in his head.

My love, my actions, and my example can encourage people of all faiths to be the best that they can be. That is the answer, really, he mused. If I am being the best that I can be in Christianity, then I need to act like Jesus. That seems pretty simple really. Jesus would love everyone, he would not be fearful or mean and he would not allow rumors and falsehoods to be directed towards another.

Tim knew what he had to do. He picked up the phone and dialed.

Doug was resting on the couch in Lucy's living room while she took some time to work on her book. His phone buzzed in his pocket. To his dismay, it was the church calling. He nearly let it go to voice mail, but decided at the last minute that he was ready to confront Pastor Jones.

"Hello?"

"Hi Doug, this is Pastor Jones. I am calling to remind you that we have board meeting in a half an hour. Will you be joining us?"

Doug had completely forgot about the meeting. "Oh, um, I don't know. I'm not sure if I am welcome."

"Of course you are Doug. Please, I need your help. I know that I don't deserve it right now, but I need to talk to Lucy. Do you think you can convince her to come to the meeting tonight with you?"

"Why, so you can humiliate her some more? No, I think that she has been through enough." Doug could feel his temper rising.

"I can see why you would think that. I'm so sorry Doug. All I can really say is that I have finally begun to understand Lucy. I need to make things right somehow. Please, can you bring her?" The Pastor pleaded.

Doug sighed, wondering if he could trust the Pastor. "I will talk to her, but I'm not making any promises, okay?"

"That is all I can ask of you. Thank you Doug, goodbye."

Doug entered Lucy's office looking worried. "Lucy, the Pastor just called to remind me of board meeting in a few minutes. He made a very strange request. He wants you to come too. You don't have to though. It's perfectly fine to say no."

"Doug!" Lucy shrieked, throwing her arms around his neck. "This is great! Why would I say no? Our love is working, I can feel it!"

Doug was still worried. He knew that Lucy was full of faith and joy, but he was still feeling very protective of her. A few minutes later, they were in the car, driving to the church in silence.

Three doors down, Jason received a text. It was his dad. He said that he had read the article Jason had given him and wanted him to come down to the church immediately to discuss it. Jason wasn't sure what to think. He was afraid that his father might still be angry, but he knew that he had to go anyway.

The scene in the church conference room was very interesting. Lucy and Doug sat on one end of the long mahogany table, with Jason sitting close to Lucy. The rest of the board, 12 men from the congregation, sat at the other end of the table, chairs pushed close together in order to sit as far from Lucy as possible. When the Pastor entered the room, he surveyed the pile up of men looking suspiciously at the other end of the table. To their shock, he greeted Doug with a handshake and Lucy with a hug, along with a hug for his son.

Next he took his own seat in the center of the table, took a deep breath, and began to speak.

"Welcome, all of you, to the board meeting. I realize that we have church business to discuss, but we will be postponing that for another time. There is a much more pressing issue to discuss. I have spent the last week doing a lot of talking. I have spoken to all of you about our 'problem'. I have spoken with the police chief, Doug's boss, and many others. I have talked until I am blue in the face about fear, differences, and intolerance. Many of you have done a lot of talking too."

Some of the board members shifted uncomfortably in their seats, looking down. The Pastor continued, "I have neglected talking to someone very important, however. I have not prayed about Lucy one time. I allowed my ego to buy me into a bunch of drama and fear. I spread it out to all of you. I am here to tell you all how sorry that I am for my poor leadership."

Tim turned his attention to Doug. "We have known each other forever. I have watched you go through so many changes in your life. I know that life has not always been kind to you. I can't believe that I thought I had the right to snatch happiness away from you."

Doug felt self conscious with everyone looking at him. He finally spoke. "I am happy. When my wife died, I really didn't think that I would ever find love again. I really didn't even want it. When Lucy and I met, I wasn't looking for a relationship, but a relationship blossomed anyway. I am not here to ask anyone's permission to be happy. I have finally realized that I have that right and I don't really care what any of you think."

"You are right Doug," Tim agreed. "You don't need our permission. We have seriously overstepped our bounds. With your permission, though, I would like to continue. I have a lot of making up to do tonight."

Doug nodded, wrapping his arm around Lucy's shoulder. Lucy was surveying the energy in the room inquisitively. She could feel all kinds of emotions swirling about. There was still anger and fear, but a current of love and humility was also flowing.

"Jason, I need to thank you son." Tears welled up in Tim's eyes, his voice thick with emotion. "You have been my greatest teacher through all of this. I really don't know what I have done to deserve a son as brave and courageous as you are. You are a much bigger person than I am. This article that you gave me, it has changed me. I finally stopped for just a moment to take a long look in the mirror. I didn't like what I saw. I promise you, I am going to be spending more time at home, more time with you. I do love you son, and I want to be a good father."

Jason just nodded, overcome with emotion as well.

"I would like to share some wise words with you," Tim turned his attention back to the board members. He cleared his throat and began, *"I recognize that I am a powerful, divine being........ If more human beings understood their own vast potential to spread love and make the world a better place, can you imagine how wonderful it would be? I firmly believe that by loving instead of fearing, I can make a difference in this world. My love, my actions, and my example can encourage people of all faiths to be the best that they can be. I don't expect anyone to join me on my path, it is mine alone to follow. It is my responsibility to inspire every person that I come in contact with to walk their own path with love, compassion, and understanding. Sometimes I am misunderstood. Sometimes there are people who are stuck in fear who cannot see past our differences. That just encourages me to love more, understand more, and spread more light."*

Lucy's eyes were wide with the wonder of hearing her own words read aloud. Doug recognized them too, and held Lucy a little tighter, feeling so much pride and love for her.

"I don't know about you, but this is the kind of person I want to have in my community. I think that I can learn a lot from someone who thinks that their calling in life is to love others. In fact, I'm pretty sure that is why I chose to be a pastor."

Some of the men in the room nodded in agreement. Some still looked suspicious and uncomfortable. No one spoke.

"Lucy, I am sure that you recognize your own words. This is an excerpt from one of your books. I have no words to tell you how very sorry I am for my mean spirited behavior. I know that these are just words and that they do not take away from the fear and pain I have caused you and your families. I have no idea how I will make up for this, but I promise you that I will do every thing in my power to try.

It is my responsibility to be a good spiritual leader and I have failed miserably this time. I am determined to do better. I can't tell all of you men how to feel or what to do. I just want to challenge all of you to do a little soul searching. Pray, talk to your wives, get educated! Rocky Point is better than this. WE are better than this."

With that, the meeting adjourned. The board members filed out silently. Everyone had a lot of thinking to do.

chapter 14

"It is so good to see you Lucy!" Megan tossed her purse on the table and sat opposite her friend. "Are Tina and Amber coming?"

"Yeah, they should both be here soon," Lucy replied, taking a sip of her iced tea.

Within minutes Amber and Tina both arrived. "This is a cute little place." Amber looked around the small restaurant, taking in the French decor.

"I'm so glad everyone could make it!" Lucy hugged all of them, always thrilled to be spending time with friends. "It has been such a crazy summer, I have hardly seen you guys!"

"Speaking of crazy summer, it has been a while since you have given me an update. Is it all still torches and pitchforks in Rocky Point?" Megan knew that Lucy kept things to herself when she didn't want to upset anyone with the drama.

"Actually, no. It has been six weeks since the board meeting at the church. Things have settled down a lot. I still get a funny look at the grocery store from time to time. There are still a few neighbors who don't wave, that sort of thing. Overall though, things are so much better."

"What about the flame throwing kid? Has he given you any more trouble?"

"Oh no, Jason is a good kid. We made our peace a long time ago! Actually, he spends a fair amount of time at my house. He likes to play ball with Luke and Brian. I pay him to do yard work and odd jobs. He acts like he needs a place where he belongs. I don't think he has ever had that before."

"I'm glad that you can provide that for him Lucy. Your ability to forgive and move on is truly amazing." Tina knew that Lucy had learned the hard way to forgive. She struggled for years after her mother had abandoned her, though she rarely talked about it. "What about your new book? I know that you have had a deadline to meet. Did you make it?"

"I did! Sometimes I think this whole experience in Rocky Point was handed to me by the universe so that I could write a good book," Lucy laughed. Her book was about all religions learning to live together in peace and harmony. "I had already started the book and signed a publishing deal long before I met Doug. I guess that I just needed a little more life experience to be able to finish it."

As lunch continued on, the girls laughed and chatted about their current events. The energy was comfortable and relaxed, the way lunch with old friends ought to feel. It felt so good to Lucy to bask in the joy and peace that her friends brought with them. While the last several months had been challenging, she had managed to attract the love of her life. Doug encouraged her, loved her unconditionally and gave her kids so much love and attention.

Tina studied Lucy from across the table. Sometimes she marveled at the fact that she had raised this incredible woman. She smiled wistfully, thinking about her visit from Doug yesterday and how much Lucy's life was about to change.

"What are you smiling about?" Lucy asked, startling Tina out of her thoughts.

"Oh, nothing!" Tina knew that keeping a secret of this magnitude was going to be hard.....

About the author

KATIE WEAVER LIVES in Idaho with her husband Scott and three children, Mykah, Mataya and Marianna. She loves camping, gardening, rock hounding and spending time with her family. Katie is a radio personality and author as well as a psychic, medium and healer. She is one part of the Psychic Sisters, a title that she shares with her sisters Kristi, Kara and Ronda.

To learn more about Katie and listen to her on the radio, please visit:

www.thepsychicsisters.net

Connect with Katie on Facebook

www.facebook.com/authorkatieweaver